# HAPPINESS BY THE NUMBERS

## 9 Steps To Authentic Happiness

DR HEATHER SILVIO

Panther Books

Published in the United States by Panther Books, Las Vegas.

Contact the publisher at:
information@pantherbooks.us

Correspondence to the author may be sent to:
hlsilvio@yahoo.com

Cover design by A.L. Hinds.

This is a work of nonfiction. Information contained is based on the author's experiences as a clinical psychologist and life coach. Sources are provided for non-public domain information. Quotes are from public figures not personally known to the author; the use of the quotes does not imply endorsement by those individuals of this book.

Copyright © 2016 Heather Silvio

All rights reserved. No part of this book may be reproduced or transmitted in any form or by any means, electronic or mechanical, including photocopying, recording, or by any information storage and retrieval system, without the written permission of the publisher, except where permitted by law.

ISBN (Print) 978-0-9908005-4-5
ISBN (E-book) 978-0-9908005-5-2

## ALSO BY HEATHER SILVIO

Paranormal Talent Agency (Books 1-6)

Special Snowflake Syndrome: The Unrecognized Personality Disorder Destroying the World

Not Quite Famous: A Romantic Comedy of an Actress on the Edge

Beyond the Abyss: Tales of the Supernatural

Stress Disorders: A Healing Path for PTSD

Courting Death

# CONTENTS

| | |
|---|---|
| Acknowledgments | i |
| Introduction | 1 |
| Pre-Test | 7 |
| Step 1 Diet | 17 |
| Step 2 Physical Activity | 43 |
| Step 3 Sleep & Meditation | 71 |
| Step 4 Emotion Regulation | 87 |
| Step 5 Who Are You? | 113 |
| Step 6 Planning | 129 |
| Step 7 Community | 155 |
| Step 8 Spirituality & Mindfulness | 177 |
| Step 9 Trust | 195 |
| Final Thoughts | 217 |

# ACKNOWLEDGMENTS

To all of the patients and clients I have worked with as a licensed clinical psychologist and life coach. Without you, this book would not exist. I am forever grateful to have been even a small part of your journey.

# INTRODUCTION

Happiness is an elusive, highly subjective state of being. Yet, everyone knows it when they feel it. Happiness results from getting the "good stuff", whatever that means to you. Of course, I don't mean material good stuff (since we've all heard money can't buy happiness); no, the good stuff I refer to is whatever brings you pleasure, contentment, joy, love, bliss, satisfaction, or delight. I suspect all of us would like to experience every single one of those specific descriptors of happiness that I just used.

That's where *Happiness by the Numbers: 9 Steps to Authentic Happiness* comes in. This book offers you a step by step guide to making immediate, short-term, and long-term changes to dramatically increase your subjective sense of happiness. I organize and present the *Steps* by first introducing topics, and then providing examples, explanations, and concrete recommendations for making changes based on each topic. That's not to say that the changes in this book are easy. If it were that easy, you'd probably already be completely satisfied and you wouldn't need this book!

Having said the above, allow me to make a probably startling admission. There is nothing new in this book. There really isn't. Every idea in here has been presented before. Why, then, did I write this book? And, more importantly, why would you continue reading?

I wrote the book because I have not seen this information collected and presented in the specific way that I am doing so here. As we all know, we are bombarded on a daily basis with as many ways to help ourselves be prettier, smarter, more popular, funnier – you name the desired attribute – as there are people in the world. The problem is that with this wealth of information comes misinformation and information overload. Keep reading to cut through that information overload to focus on what works.

I decided to put together this step-by-step program based on my experience as a clinical psychologist and life coach. I know what works. I have seen the *individual* pieces of my overall program work for people; my hope and expectation for you is that you can approach the program as a *total life makeover* resulting in increased happiness. And not the temporary, "I'm simply denying I'm unhappy", sleep-walking-through-life happiness. Genuine, authentic, lasting happiness.

Let me be clear that this book is not meant to be a research thesis of any kind. My book largely contains information I have gleaned through a lifetime of exposure to the various topics, along with my opinions of the most effective way to implement changes. Therefore, the chapters will not be dotted with references. For information specifically tied to an individual or source, of course I'll give credit where credit is due, since I'm not going to take credit for others' work. This approach means a less-cluttered book for you!

If you would like more information, including additional sources or studies backing up my opinions, please feel free to do additional research. This book is meant to be approached almost like a workbook; I provide just enough information to give my practice exercises some context; I'm not trying to provide a definitive thesis! I hope you enjoy the book from this perspective, having avoided feeling bogged down by an overly scientific and academic approach.

Let me also add that I am a psychologist, not a medical doctor, so although I trained/practiced in health psychology, please, please,

please, if you are at all uncertain about any of my recommendations and how they may impact your health, ask your medical providers.

A frequent reason people have trouble being happy or finding happiness is because they focus on events outside themselves – waiting for some external change to their environment to make them happy, whether a romantic partner, a fabulous job, oodles of money, etc. The key to lasting authentic happiness is to learn more about yourself, identify your specific desires, and then focus on changing yourself instead of relying on external things or people.

Happiness comes from healthiness in *Body*, *Mind*, and *Spirit*. In this program there are three *Steps* within each of these three areas. The *9 Steps* in total will thus offer a step by step program to help you achieve balance and healthiness in all three broader areas. As I stated above, I designed the book like a workbook, asking lots of questions so you can learn and explore alternative ways of thinking and doing. These alternatives will be suggestions to try to see if something works better for you. There will be many exercises for you to practice what I present.

Each *Step*'s chapter has a vignette demonstrating the application of that *Step*'s guidance with a former client of mine [though identifying information naturally has been changed for privacy and confidentiality]. Each chapter ends with a Chapter Purpose paragraph and a recap of the offered practice exercises. My hope is that if you didn't do the practice exercises during the chapter, the reminder at the end will motivate you! As I always tell my clients – if you don't make changes or otherwise implement what you learn, you will stay where you are.

As you read through the below overview of my program, I want to note that everyone is an individual and there's no such thing as perfection. If you have chronic health problems or physical limitations, for example, that impact your ability to implement the first two steps, boost or improve as much as possible and remember all forward progress is to be celebrated!

## *9 Steps to Authentic Happiness*: An Overview

**Part 1 Body**: Step 1 Diet

Physical health is essential to overall wellbeing and happiness. In this chapter, I discuss the roles of balanced eating, emotional eating, alcohol consumption, and hydration on health. There will be several practice exercises intended to help you self-assess and implement changes.

### Step 2 Physical Activity

Next the focus shifts to how physical activity is critical for optimal health in body, mind, and spirit. In this chapter, I discuss healthy weight, levels and types of exercise, and the importance of motivation in making physical lifestyle changes.

### Step 3 Sleep & Meditation

As the final chapter under the *Body* heading, I cover sleep and meditation for rejuvenation; this is somewhat of a bridge step to *Part 2 Mind*. By the end of the chapter, you'll better understand your own sleep patterns and will have the opportunity to practice meditation.

**Part 2 Mind**: Step 4 Emotion Regulation

A critical component of true happiness is awareness of our self-talk and whether it is helping or hurting our wellbeing. In this chapter, I discuss use of cognitive behavioral therapy and positive psychology techniques to modify our self-talk. I close the chapter with a discussion of the impact of self-confidence.

### Step 5 Who Are You?

Authenticity necessitates challenging you to consider whether who-you-are is who-you-want-to-be. This involves considering authenticity within yourself, finding your purpose, developing a life plan in support of that purpose, and taking those initial steps, whether big or small, in support of that plan.

## Step 6 Planning

If you don't have a plan to accomplish your goals, it really is just wishful thinking with little chance of success. As planning is the process by which you can accomplish your goals, I describe goal-setting and development, effective time management, and the role of motivation in our goal development and achievement.

## **Part 3 Spirit** : Step 7 Community

Returning to the topic of positive psychology, I discuss the importance of a meaningful life in being happy and increasing your sense of belonging in the world. The importance of volunteering for both personal and community development concludes the chapter.

## Step 8 Spirituality & Mindfulness

Beginning with a bold statement that spirituality is vital to happiness, I first define religious spirituality and secular spirituality. Taking a broader view of spiritual connection, I then discuss mindfulness, minimalism, and gratitude as methods for connecting with ourselves and others.

## Step 9 Trust

I conclude the *9 Steps* with the idea that trust is at the core of human society. I offer guidance and specific recommendations on ways to build trust in yourself and with others, including recognizing the role of taking others' perspectives and learning to forgive ourselves and others.

## Program Length

If you simply read this book, you will gain knowledge and start looking more closely at your thoughts and choices; however, this will provide only the minimum amount of change and increased happiness. If you actively work the program, *Step* by *Step*, answering the questions and doing the practice exercises, it will take a minimum of 18 weeks – and for the most benefit, closer to six months. You can always start with the minimum and then reread the book, actually working the program. I've certainly done that before with self-help and how-to guidance. If you're interested in a more guided program with me, contact me at hlsilvio@yahoo.com.

Let me end this introduction with two final thoughts I often share with my patients and clients:

### Happiness is a choice.

### Dreams are the reality you have yet to create.

# PRE-TEST

The pre-test will help you determine just how happy and healthy you truly are across a number of domains, or life areas. Your answers will suggest which of the three broader areas, as well as which of the nine *Steps* encompassed, you could most focus on.

## How Happy Are You?

Each question is presented with four possible answers. There are no right or wrong answers. As you read each question, mark the answer that seems to leap out at you. Do not over-think the items. There are no trick questions. The purpose of the pre-test is to help you, so allow it to do so by approaching it with an open mind and allowing your gut reactions to take center stage. For now, ignore the numbers next to each question.

1. How happy or content do you feel? (4)
    - A   Completely unhappy or discontented
    - B   Happy fewer days than not
    - C   Happy more days than not
    - D   Completely happy or content

2. How varied is your exercise routine? (2)
   A   I don't exercise
   B   I do the same thing every time with no variation
   C   Occasionally I'll do something different
   D   I do a mix of cardio, weights, and flexibility exercises regularly

3. Are you able to stay focused during activities? (8)
   A   No, I'm stuck in the past or worried about the future
   B   Maybe, but I'm easily distracted during activities
   C   Sometimes, when it's an activity I enjoy
   D   Absolutely! I regularly take time to savor life

4. How often do you wake up feeling refreshed? (3)
   A   Never
   B   Sometimes
   C   Often
   D   Always

5. How satisfied are you with your current weight? (1)
   A   Not at all
   B   Some
   C   Very
   D   Completely

6. Do you make lists? (6)
   A   Why?
   B   If I think about it
   C   For limited things, like groceries
   D   For everything, so nothing gets missed

7. Do you have emotional support (family/friends/partner)? (7)
   A   I don't need emotional support
   B   I only have acquaintances
   C   I have a few deeper friends
   D   I have family/friends/partner that I truly love (or at least like a lot!)

8. Do you have gut reactions to people, situations, or choices? (9)
   A   No
   B   Yes, but I never go with them
   C   Yes, I frequently listen to what my instincts are saying
   D   I rely on my gut reactions for a true gauge of my feelings

9. How often do you experience total absorption in an activity because you love it? (5)
   A   I wish
   B   Occasionally
   C   Frequently
   D   I'm in the zone more than I'm not

10. How would you describe your alcohol consumption? (1)
    A   Drink to excess most times I drink
    B   Moderate but frequent drinking
    C   One or two drinks one or two nights per week
    D   Never or minimally

11. How physically active are you day to day? (2)
    A   Mostly I sit
    B   Fairly sedentary, but sometimes take the stairs
    C   Try to hit the gym once in awhile plus low key everyday stuff, like gardening
    D   Regular exercising plus multiple activities indoors and out

12. How would you describe your confidence in yourself? (4)

    A   Completely lacking
    B   Lack confidence in many areas
    C   Confident more than not
    D   Quite confident

13. Do you alter your personality in different situations? (5)

    A   I'm a total actor/actress
    B   My colleagues wouldn't recognize me with my friends
    C   I have situational awareness and can modify as needed
    D   I make only minor changes to how I present myself in different scenarios

14. How many people in your life do you truly trust? (9)

    A   None
    B   A few
    C   Many
    D   I trust people until they give me a reason not to

15. How often do you volunteer? (7)

    A   Isn't working for free the definition of slavery?
    B   I'd like to, but I just don't have time
    C   A couple of times a year, I try to give back
    D   At least a couple of times each month

16. How often do you exercise? (2)

    A   Um, never
    B   1-2 times per week for 30 minutes or less
    C   3-4 times per week for 30-60 minutes
    D   Every day for at least 30 minutes

17. What are your thoughts on owning stuff? (8)
    A   The more I can buy, the happier I am
    B   It's hard for me to find stuff in the clutter of my home
    C   I try to set limits but still own more than I'd prefer
    D   I own only what has meaning to me and I rarely if ever make impulsive purchases

18. How physically healthy do you feel? (1)
    A   Completely unhealthy
    B   Healthy fewer days than not
    C   Healthy more days than not
    D   Completely healthy

19. Do you have well-thought out plans for the future? (6)
    A   Die young and leave a good-looking corpse
    B   I have vague ideas about what I'd like to do
    C   I'm good for the next 3-6 months
    D   I know exactly what I want now, next year, in five years, and I know exactly how to get it

20. How often does it take you longer than 30 minutes to fall asleep at night? (3)
    A   Every single night
    B   More nights than not
    C   Rarely but more than I'd like
    D   Almost never

21. Do you admit mistakes? (9)
    A   I don't make mistakes
    B   I try to
    C   Most of the time
    D   Absolutely – nobody's perfect

22. How often do you do fun activities? (4)

    A   Never
    B   I try but it's hard to find the time
    C   Fairly often
    D   Every single day

23. Are you satisfied with your level of spirituality? (8)

    A   No
    B   A little bit
    C   Quite a bit
    D   Completely

24. Are you organized? (6)

    A   Not in the least
    B   I know where things are most of the time
    C   I have a plan and usually follow it
    D   I plan, organize, color code; I will do anything and everything, whatever it takes!

25. Do you like your job? (5)

    A   Not at all
    B   Sometimes
    C   Most of the time
    D   Best job ever

26. How connected do you feel to your community? (7)

    A   No connection at all
    B   I know my neighbors to say hi
    C   I participate in the occasional 5K or community dinner
    D   I am active in the community quite a bit

27. Do you meditate or otherwise slow down to focus? (3)
   A   No, I have no interest/time
   B   I've tried, unsuccessfully
   C   I do occasionally
   D   Frequently

For now, continuing to ignore the number in parentheses after each question, score the quiz, using the following guide:

For every A answer, give yourself 0 points = \_\_\_\_\_
For every B answer, give yourself 1 point = \_\_\_\_\_
For every C answer, give yourself 2 points = \_\_\_\_\_
For every D answer, give yourself 3 points = \_\_\_\_\_

Add the points together for your total score. Based on your responses to the 27 questions, what is your **Global Level of Happiness (0-81)?** \_\_\_\_\_

55-81   *Why are you reading this book?* I'm kidding, of course. If you scored in this range, clearly you are doing a lot that works well for you. Check your individual responses (see below) to determine if there are specific *Steps* where you would most benefit from making changes. I would still recommend reading the entire program for more options to increase your happiness.

28-54   *Middle of the road, huh?* If you scored in this range, your responses suggest one of two things. You are middle of the road in everything, or you have a mixture of successful and less successful areas that are essentially cancelling each other out. Consider your individual responses to determine which one fits you, but in either instance, I am confident you could learn a thing or two from each *Step*.

0-27    *Glass half-empty defines your world view!* If you scored in this range, don't despair. It may seem like you have a lot of work to do, but all this means is that you have an exciting time ahead of you as you begin the program. I recommend also reviewing your individual responses to determine if you have specific areas of strength from which to build further success.

Now that you know your **Global Level of Happiness**, I'd like you to consider your individual scores. This will allow you to determine areas of greatest strength as well as areas most in need of development. This may help guide you in the ways described above, though I would still recommend reading the entire book from start to finish, as it is a step by step program.

The number in parentheses after each question corresponds to its particular *Step*. There are three questions per *Step*. Use the scoring method above to determine your *Step* scores:

For every A answer, give yourself 0 points
For every B answer, give yourself 1 point
For every C answer, give yourself 2 points
For every D answer, give yourself 3 points

Add up your scores for the three items in each *Step* and place them below (0-9 for each *Step*):
Step 1 Diet = _____
Step 2 Physical Activity = _____
Step 3 Sleep & Meditation = _____
Step 4 Emotion Regulation = _____
Step 5 Who Are You? = _____
Step 6 Planning = _____
Step 7 Community = _____
Step 8 Spirituality & Mindfulness = _____
Step 9 Trust = _____

The numbers above can help you in two ways.

First, consider the *Step* score totals:

*If your *Step* total is between 0-3, this is an area significantly in need of development and the corresponding chapters can be considered for guidance on substantial changes.

*If your *Step* total is between 4-6, this is an area where you're doing okay but can improve by reading the corresponding chapters and making moderate changes.

*If your *Step* total is between 7-9, this is an area of excellence for you and the corresponding chapters can be used to increase your satisfaction in the area.

Second, you can rank order your *Step* totals if you'd like to approach the program in a slightly different way, by either focusing on areas of strength first to build further confidence before tackling areas of greater need, or by working with your lowest score totals first to see more obvious changes. Either option is great, as is, of course, simply reading through and working the *Steps* in order!

## DR. HEATHER SILVIO

# PART 1
# BODY

## STEP 1
## DIET

*Tell me what you eat and I will tell you what you are.*
Anthelme Brillat-Savarin (19th century French food writer)

The above quote is the origin of the oft repeated phrase, "you are what you eat", and thus is the perfect beginning to this chapter on eating. Let me start with a definition – a diet simply means what you're eating, not a specific plan of eating to lose weight. There is mostly no right or wrong way to any specific diet (although if you're only eating one thing, like cabbage, that's probably not so good). The key is how it makes you feel – and this includes doctor's testing of cholesterol, etc! In other words, you can't just eat cookies all day because they're yummy.

Do you feel energized throughout your day? Or do you feel like you're two steps from a coma? You need a diet that satisfies, helps you achieve weight goals, and is healthy. There are many research studies suggesting this or that diet is superior to all others, but honestly, statistics can be manipulated.

The purpose of this section is not to tell you how to eat. The purpose is to start you thinking about what you put in your body, and whether it is consistent with your beliefs, the most helpful and healthful option, and ultimately sustainable over the long term. This chapter will be the beginning of your food journey.

## Achieving a Healthy Weight

*Why is it important?*

This question probably seems like one of those "well, duh" questions, but I think it's important to specifically state that being overweight or obese puts tremendous pressure on the body. Maintaining a healthy weight avoids the risk of a variety of medical issues. Plus, frankly, most people just feel better at a healthy weight.

*How do you do it?*

The remainder of this section describes various ways to evaluate and then make dietary changes to help you achieve the fine balance between taking in enough energy to function optimally without taking in excess that results in unwanted pounds. It's pretty straightforward.

> Weight gain occurs when you take in more calories than you burn.

No matter what other factors you consider, this is the basic truth. If you are one of those rare individuals who want to gain weight, you will need to eat more – though do it healthfully! If you like your current weight, then you are clearly balancing your calorie intake and expenditure fairly well. You may want to read the rest of this chapter to see if you would like to modify your dietary lifestyle to simply be healthier. If you are overweight, you will want to read the rest of this chapter with an eye toward identifying a new approach to eating and exercise. But first let's find out where you are in your dietary patterns.

*What are dietary patterns?*

You likely already know whether you need to gain, maintain, or lose weight, but you may not know exactly why, or have an idea of the nutrition content of your diet. We are going to spend some time figuring out exactly where you stand, so to speak, so you can begin to make positive changes. What I want you to do is simple:

## Practice Exercise – Food Diary

Go out and get a small notebook; the little spiral kind seems to work the best, but another option is the electronic notes on your smart phone. (On the next page in this book, I've included a sample page you can photocopy, if you prefer.)

For the next two weeks, I want you to write down every single time food or drink passes your lips. Note that the reason I ask for two weeks' monitoring is that one week may catch a bunch of anomalous eating choices, where two weeks invariably captures how you truly eat or drink. You'll want to chart at least the following:

- When you're eating or drinking.
- What you're eating or drinking, including:
    - Portion size.
    - Calorie estimation (e.g., use a free calorie counter on sites like myfitnesspal.com).
- How you feel after eating.

## Helpful Hint

If you have three M-n-Ms courtesy of your officemate – write it down. You go to the local Chinese buffet for dinner – write down every trip to the buffet line. You take a Zumba class – write down how much water you drink before, during, and after the class. Everything. Do this and then continue reading.

# Food Diary

Day of the week / Date / Time: _____
Food / Drink consumed: _____
Portion size / Estimated calories: _____
How do you feel after eating? _____

Day of the week / Date / Time: _____
Food / Drink consumed: _____
Portion size / Estimated calories: _____
How do you feel after eating? _____

Day of the week / Date / Time: _____
Food / Drink consumed: _____
Portion size / Estimated calories: _____
How do you feel after eating? _____

Day of the week / Date / Time: _____
Food / Drink consumed: _____
Portion size / Estimated calories: _____
How do you feel after eating? _____

Day of the week / Date / Time: _____
Food / Drink consumed: _____
Portion size / Estimated calories: _____
How do you feel after eating? _____

Day of the week / Date / Time: _____
Food / Drink consumed: _____
Portion size / Estimated calories: _____
How do you feel after eating? _____

*What do you do with your Food Diary?*

Now, I want you to continue reading this chapter, keeping your Food Diary near at hand, so that you can review what you've written and group like-items together as you read about food groups and proper nutrition. I want you to analyze your diet according to nutritional recommendations and see where you are doing well and where you maybe need a little boost. Ready? Let's review some of the basics that apply no matter what your dietary lifestyle, and establish concrete steps you can take to improve your dietary health.

## The Basics
### (courtesy of the USDA's ChooseMyPlate website)

Why am I starting with the USDA recommendations? Yes, there are tons of specialty diets out there, recommending eliminating certain types of food for optimal health (and I briefly mention some of these later). However, in my experience working with patients and clients, following the below guidelines has worked quite well for them. For that reason, I'm starting with the national guidelines. This is just a place to start; you may do better with a more specialized diet.

Food groups. All of us remember the food pyramid. Well, it has transformed into MyPlate. You use a place setting visual to determine how to balance your intake from the food groups: fruits, vegetables, grains, protein, dairy, and oils (not a group, per se). MyPlate presents the concept of a healthy diet, emphasizing fruits and vegetables for about half your diet and whole grains and protein foods for the other half; fat-free or low-fat dairy products round out a diet that ideally is low in saturated fats, trans fats, cholesterol, salt, and added sugars. From this definition of a healthy diet, the government recommends staying within your daily calorie needs by making smart choices from each of the food groups.

Exact recommendations vary according to age, sex, and activity level, so I won't be delving into that here; however, one easy rule of thumb is to make sure there is some kind of a fruit or vegetable, grain product, and protein food in every one of your meals, and that all of your snacks include a fruit or vegetable.

## Practice Exercise – Nutrient Needs

Take a look at your food diary. It is critical to be certain your consumption meets the general dietary recommendations so that your essential nutrient needs are met. Do your meals and snacks meet my rule of thumb described above? Consider breaking out each day:

### Breakfast
Protein _____
Grain _____
Fruit/Vegetable _____

### Lunch
Protein _____
Grain _____
Fruit/Vegetable _____

### Dinner
Protein _____
Grain _____
Fruit/Vegetable _____

### Snacks
Protein _____
Grain _____
Fruit/Vegetable _____

If your meals and snacks do not include a protein, grain, and fruit/vegetable, consider where you can add more in.

## Helpful Hints

- Add a glass of 100% fruit juice to a meal.
- Have a piece of fruit with your snack.
- Utilize visual reminders, for example, placing a printout of a list of representative foods from a needed group (like vegetables) on your refrigerator, so that you think about stocking up when you go grocery shopping or choosing one when you are reaching for a snack.

Portion sizes. The majority of people get tripped up here. Almost everyone eats more than they think – which is probably why they don't lose weight, despite their fervent belief they are eating less! A serving size isn't the amount you've chosen to eat; it's the amount equal to what has been labeled a serving size of a specific food item with respect to the number of calories and nutrients it contains. When eating out or getting take out, this is a huge danger; one method for managing it is to immediately cut your food in half and save the rest for another meal.

Nutrient rich foods. The amount of nutrients in your food won't make much of a difference in terms of your weight if you're still eating a whole lot more calories than you're burning off. However, certain healthier foods, like high protein foods and whole wheat bread products, can help you stay full longer and thus eat less overall. Ideally, you want nutrient dense foods, or foods with more nutrients per calorie than other choices within the same food group. Learn to read the labels on your packaged foods and research the most healthful preparations when cooking.

Manage your weight. As stated, whatever your weight goal, you can manage it in part by being aware of your food choices and making changes where needed. Using SuperTracker on ChooseMyPlate.gov, you can create a profile so that you can be provided with a detailed diet plan tailored specifically for you. It not only analyzes your diet and provides nutrition information, but also healthy eating tips, information about food groups, weight loss information, and tips on planning a healthy menu.

*What can you do right now?*

Having analyzed your diet and made simple changes to increase (or decrease) areas according to your need, let's get a little more in the weeds.

## Practice Exercise – Planning Your Meals

1) Do you have a cookbook? Yes? Okay, great. If not, can you borrow one, check one out at the library, or buy one? You can also get recipes off of the web. In any event, I want you to start a collection of recipes to try – there are pretty basic ones, if this is an area that is completely foreign to you – so that you can try a new recipe every week. Experiment! A great option is to make a big batch of something (like chili) on the weekend to use all week.

2) Based on these recipes, your food diary, and your identified nutrition needs, I want you to learn how to plan menus and grocery shop with an itemized list. If this seems overwhelming, there are apps and websites that offer assistance (e.g., WebMD offers a free online service, as does the mobile app Pepperplate).

## Dietary Lifestyle Possibilities

When it comes to dietary lifestyle choices, what you eat may be about a whole lot more than just meeting nutritional needs. After evaluating your current eating habits and making certain you're at least getting the nutrients your body requires for optimal functioning, the next step is to determine if you're otherwise happy with your choices.

## Practice Exercise – Dietary Lifestyle

As noted above, what we eat can be about much more that just whether or not we're getting specific nutrient needs met and at the appropriate portion sizes. What we eat is often a reflection of who we are and what we need/want. Take a few minutes to answer the following to help you determine whether or not your dietary lifestyle choices are working for you in this broader sense:

- Do your food choices reflect your personal ethical beliefs?
- Do your food choices reflect management of allergies or sensitivities?
- Do you need to respond to specific medical issues, like high cholesterol or diabetes?
- Do you need to gain or lose weight?
- Do you want the structure of goals and guidance to follow when trying to make changes for any of the above?

The above questions may help you determine what dietary lifestyle choices may be more effective for you. I don't endorse any of the lifestyle choices over another, but they may spark something:

- Vegetarian: not consuming meat, fish, or poultry (yes, this includes seafood, but no, it does not include cheese; see below).
- Vegan: not consuming any animal product like meat, cheese, dairy, or eggs.
- Low Calorie Diet: ingesting 1000-1800 calories/day or 10-25% fewer calories than the "average" diet.
- Low Fat Diet: keeping overall fat under 30% of the daily caloric intake, with saturated fats kept at less than 10%, monounsaturated fats to less than 15%, and polyunsaturated to less than 10% of your daily caloric intake.

- Low Carbohydrate Diet: staying between 50-150 grams initially then lowering to between 20-30 grams of carbohydrates per day.
- High Protein Diet: consuming protein as 10-35% of calorie intake, though some recommend a flat 120 grams.
- Paleolithic, or paleo, diet: ingesting only food that our ancient ancestors likely would have eaten, such as meat, and excluding foods that had not been developed, such as dairy and refined/processed foods.
- Gluten-free: excluding foods with gluten, such as found in wheat, barley, and rye.

I'd like to make a brief note about food allergies and food sensitivities. The gluten-free diet was originally intended for those facing celiac disease but many others have claimed to feel better on a similar diet. The fact is that a person can have allergies and/or food sensitivities, whether to gluten, dairy, nuts, etc. Testing in a doctor's office may help discover some of those. Paying attention to how you feel after consuming food may help you discover others. But, if you really want to determine this, one of the best ways that I've seen is to try an elimination diet.

## (Optional) Practice Exercise – Elimination Diet

This is optional, based on how you are feeling after eating, despite the changes you've already made to your diet. An elimination diet can be simple or complex, depending on how you wish to tackle it.

- A simple elimination diet: Have you noticed feeling better or worse when you've eaten or not eaten certain foods? Eliminate that food for 2-4 weeks. For example, I noticed that I felt ill after eating eggs. When I got allergy testing, it showed I was allergic to, among other things, chicken. Could that mean I had a sensitivity to eggs? Who knows? What I tried was not eating eggs for about a month and then having some...I felt terrible, which was reason enough for me to mostly eliminate eggs from my diet.

- A more complex elimination diet: Try eliminating gluten, dairy, sugar, and alcohol for 2-4 weeks. How do you feel? Based on that you can either stop there, or add items back in one at a time to see where the sensitivities may be. In any event, this is a tougher option, but I've seen some pretty amazing results.

## Overall Dietary Lifestyle Recommendations

In sum, although the above dietary choices are offered as options for lifestyle choices, I recognize that many people reading are most interested, at least in the short-term, in weight loss capabilities. As mentioned prior, losing weight seems to be quite simple – expend more energy than you take in. Of course, folks who have struggled with their weight know that it's not really that simple in terms of implementation. The above has been offered in the hopes that you will find the right dietary lifestyle for you – one that helps you achieve or maintain specific weight goals, offers sufficient nutrients to remain healthy, and that works with you personally, such that you enjoy what you're eating, you aren't hungry all the time, and you don't feel sick because of an imbalance in the types of food you're choosing.

## Emotional Eating

I can hear you now, if it were just that easy to change your eating habits, you would have done so. And, of course, you're absolutely right. That's where this next section comes into play. Emotional eating can potentially make dietary lifestyle changes quite difficult.

*What is emotional eating?*

Simply put – eating in response to feelings or emotions instead of hunger. These feelings can run the gamut from anger, anxiety, boredom, sadness, loneliness, frustration, or even happiness, joy, and love. These feelings can result from major life events (like a wedding), the day-to-day buildup of frustration (road rage, anyone?), and/or underlying mental health issues. Whatever the cause, an increase in negative emotions may result in emotional eating. I've even seen statistics reporting that up to 75% of the food we consume may be unrelated to hunger!

*Why would you eat food when you're not hungry?*

When the feelings are negative, consider that comfort food has that name for a purpose. Whether fried foods, sugary sweets, or salty snacks, somewhere along the way, we learned we feel better, at least in the short-term, when we eat these foods. When the feelings are positive, well, then we're just enjoying the moment with our friends and family! Food is an integral part of celebration, right? We eat in celebration of happy occasions, like promotions or engagements. What about when we eat just because the food is there? That is situational eating and, in my experience, often goes along with eating due to boredom. Someone brings donuts to work and even though you had a filling breakfast, you seemingly can't help but eat one. After all, who turns down chocolate covered pastries?

*What do you do if you emotionally eat?*

The good news is that all habits can be broken and that's what emotional eating, at its core, really is – a habitual response to emotions. Although certainly challenging, habits can be broken. By breaking the emotional eating habit, you can not only maintain your healthy dietary lifestyle, but you can also learn to manage the negative emotions and to handle the difficult situations that simply would have returned after you finished eating that package of ding-dongs.

## Practice Exercise – Uncovering Emotional Eating

Identifying your own personal triggers is the first step. Remember your food diary? One of the easiest ways to identify your triggers is to repeat the food diary exercise for another two weeks, but without including portion size or calorie estimates, and adding in thoughts and feelings, as described below.

1. Record what you are doing, thinking, and feeling when you eat. Every time you eat or drink anything, pull out that notebook and write (see sample below you can photocopy, if you prefer):
    a. Date, time, and situation.
    b. Your immediate thoughts and feelings.
    c. Whether you're actually hungry.

## Emotional Eating Diary

Day of the week / Date / Time: _____
Food / Drink consumed: _____
What am I thinking and feeling?: _____
Am I actually hungry? _____

Day of the week / Date / Time: _____
Food / Drink consumed: _____
What am I thinking and feeling?: _____
Am I actually hungry? _____

Day of the week / Date / Time: _____
Food / Drink consumed: _____
What am I thinking and feeling?: _____
Am I actually hungry? _____

At the end of two weeks, review what you've recorded and look for patterns. You will undoubtedly be able to identify your emotional eating patterns.

2. Make immediate changes in your environment based on the results of Step 1. Remove temptations but don't deprive yourself. What this means is:
    a. If you know you can't see a bag of Oreos without eating half, don't keep them in the house.
    b. However, don't eliminate all "bad" or unhealthy foods from your diet – this simply sets you up for failure later when you give in to the inevitable cravings.
    c. Keep healthy snacks on hand.
    d. If you reflect on how you're feeling and you're not experiencing negative emotions, if you just really want a cookie, then have a cookie.
    e. Also, we tend to eat more when we're tired or thirsty, so keep plenty of water on hand and try for eight hours of sleep per night.
3. Accomplish short-term changes that halt the emotional eating. This primarily involves engaging in a distracting activity until the urge to eat ceases:
    a. The more active the choice, the better, because it involves your entire body; options like walking, bicycling, or dancing.
    b. But, sedentary distractions work too; these include reading, listening to music, or taking a bubble bath.
    c. Since we are social creatures, involving others in your distracting activity, such as going out with a friend, would be a great option. Assuming you don't go out to eat!
4. Learn to manage the root causes of emotional eating, especially stress, more effectively:
    a. On your own you can try yoga, meditation, or

diaphragmatic breathing (described later in this book) to reduce your elevated stress level.

b. If you find this ineffective, or if you have a fair idea that there are significant underlying emotional issues, not just difficulties coping with stress, you may wish to consider individual or group therapy.

Note: Sometimes people balk at the idea of therapy – only "crazy" people need therapy – but I've found it helpful working with my own patients to explain that nobody is perfect and everyone needs assistance sometimes. A therapist can help you identify the motivation behind your choices (including emotional eating), as well as provide skills and guidance to help you back on your mentally healthy path.

Remember, as with any newly forming habit, there will be times when we slip back into our old ways of doing. If you order a pizza with everything on it because you had a fight with your spouse, that's okay. Dwelling on this perceived failure will accomplish nothing. Forgive yourself, consider a healthier way to respond in the future, and start anew the next day. If you take nothing else from this section (or this book for that matter), take this: focus on the positive. Focus on your successes and reframe so-called failures as challenges to learn from.

A sometimes forgotten component of making changes is rewarding yourself for doing well. As you begin to notice that you're eating only when hungry, reward yourself. What are rewards you would find motivating, that are doable? This can be as small as getting a massage, or as big as taking a European vacation. The reasoning is that we tend to repeat reinforced behaviors; so reinforce yourself! Eventually the changes will become your new habits, but this time they'll be habits you want to keep.

## Alcohol – Healthy or Evil?

Alcohol is such an interesting topic, especially from a healthy living perspective. Most people have an opinion about the stuff. Love it or hate it, since prohibition failed, alcohol's probably not going anywhere!

*What exactly is alcohol?*
No discussion can start without first establishing just what the heck alcohol even is. The simple definition is that ethyl alcohol (or ethanol) is an intoxicant found in beer, wine, and liquor, produced by the fermentation of yeast, sugars, and starches.

Alcohol impacts your entire body when consumed; overall it is a central nervous system depressant. You may feel more lively and rambunctious when drinking because alcohol lowers inhibitions, but it is not actually a stimulant. If you drink, you know the intensity of the effect of alcohol is directly proportional to the amount you consume and in what timeframe. This is because the liver can only metabolize a specific amount at a time.

How much is a standard drink? This is a great question, because frequently people will say they only had one drink, which may technically be true, but if it was, say, a giant margarita at their favorite Mexican restaurant, odds are that drink had more than one shot of liquor in it. And thus they didn't truly have only one drink. What you're looking at is one 12-oz beer, 8-oz malt liquor, 5 oz wine, and 1.5 oz of distilled liquor (like tequila) all being about the same. It doesn't matter what else it comes wrapped in and whether it has a tiny umbrella; these standard amounts equal one drink.

*How come some people can drink like fish?*
Ah, the age old question. Why can some people drink for days without apparent effect and others, like yours truly, are tipsy on one and really need to stop at two? As you might imagine, there are many

variables that determine an individual's response to alcohol. Age, gender, physical condition, race, and ethnicity all play a role in the response to the consumption of alcohol. Naturally, situational factors also influence an individual's response – how quickly was the alcohol consumed and was any food consumed. Oh yeah, and if you're on certain medications, that can increase the impact of alcohol. Or kill you. Really, you shouldn't drink if you're on certain medications (or pregnant, for that matter) – check the labels and with your doctor.

*What's considered a little, too much, or just enough alcohol?*

Just like individuals have opinions about alcohol, so do various stakeholder groups. There are no set amounts of what's considered good, bad, or indecent. For moderate drinking, a general rule of thumb is to limit yourself to one drink per hour, but not worry as much about the overall amount. If you're watching an entire day's worth of football, having 6 beers over those 6 hours is unlikely to incapacitate. But, this also assumes you aren't doing this every single day! That's the caveat. If you drink multiple days per week, then stick with at most only 1 (for women) or 2 (for men) a day.

## Practice Exercise – Alcohol Consumption (if you drink at all)

How much do you drink, in what circumstances, and how do you feel before, during, and after? For two weeks, track your alcohol consumption, noting (fillable log shown on the next page):
- Day / Date / Situation.
- Feelings before.
- Drinks consumed.
- Feelings during.
- Immediately physically after.
- Feelings immediately after.
- Physically the next day.
- Feelings the next day.

DR. HEATHER SILVIO

# Alcohol Consumption Diary

Day / Date / Time: _____
Situation & Drinks Consumed: _____
How did I feel emotionally before drinking?: _____
How do I feel physically immediately after?: _____
How do I feel physically the next day?: _____
How do I feel emotionally the next day?: _____

Day / Date / Time: _____
Situation & Drinks Consumed: _____
How did I feel emotionally before drinking?: _____
How do I feel physically immediately after?: _____
How do I feel physically the next day?: _____
How do I feel emotionally the next day?: _____

Day / Date / Time: _____
Situation & Drinks Consumed: _____
How did I feel emotionally before drinking?: _____
How do I feel physically immediately after?: _____
How do I feel physically the next day?: _____
How do I feel emotionally the next day?: _____

Day / Date / Time: _____
Situation & Drinks Consumed: _____
How did I feel emotionally before drinking?: _____
How do I feel physically immediately after?: _____
How do I feel physically the next day?: _____
How do I feel emotionally the next day?: _____

Did your alcohol consumption result in positive or negative emotional and physical feelings?

The above may certainly be challenging, and may involve a bit of retroactively trying to remember how you felt, for example, before and during drinking. However, this provides additional information about whether or not alcohol consumption is a health issue for you. If you notice excessive drinking or significant negative emotional and/or physical reactions, I would strongly recommend you speak with someone you trust and/or a professional.

*What is the bottom line?*

If you like alcohol and your practice exercise above suggests it's not a problem, feel free to continue to imbibe moderate amounts in a responsible way. If you don't particularly enjoy the taste or like the effects, I would suggest eliminating or reducing it and comparing the results.

## The Most Precious Stuff on Earth

Yep, I'm referring to water. I don't think I need to belabor the point that water is essential to human life. If we don't drink water, we die. It really is as simple as that. Where it starts getting complicated is in determining how much water to drink for optimal health. And there definitely aren't any quick easily agreed upon answers to that question! So, let's start with the easier stuff...

Water makes up the majority of your body weight and is critical to the function of every single body system. This is why even mild dehydration can have such a deleterious effect on how we're feeling – fatigue, dry mouth, headache, and muscle cramping are all signs of dehydration.

*How much should you drink?*

Now for the more complicated question. We've all heard the recommendation of 6-8 glasses of water per day. But how much is a glass? Does it matter if I'm male or female, 100 pounds or 200 pounds? What if I'm an athlete in training? Clearly there is a lot more that goes into consideration of an answer to that seemingly innocent question.

Let's start with average water lost per day. We all lose water daily through the basic functions of our body, including breathing, perspiring, and going to the bathroom. These three functions result, on average, in an individual losing about 10 cups of water per day. So, to start, you want to make sure you're at least replenishing that lost fluid. Food you consume, especially fruit, will replenish a certain percentage, approximately 20%, of that lost water. Putting aside needing additional water based on amount of exercising, you're looking at 8-9 cups of water, depending on your environment (if you live in hot, arid Las Vegas, for example, you'd better be drinking more water).

*What else impacts your water needs?*
Besides locale, the biggest impact on your water needs is directly related to your level of physical activity. Any activity that makes you sweat is a physical activity – not just "exercise" per se. The exact amount of additional water to drink is dependent on the intensity and duration of your activity, as well as how sweaty you become. If you're exercising longer than an hour, then a sports drink with its electrolyte replacement may be preferable, but otherwise drinking water is your best bet.

Beyond physical activity and environment, your personal physical condition influences how much water you need daily. Certain health conditions, like the flu, may result in lost fluids that need to be replaced. Others, like liver disease, may require you limit your fluid intake. When pregnant or breast feeding, you're likely to need additional water to stay properly hydrated. Consult your doctor of course, but recommendations range from 10-13 cups per day.

*Does it have to be water?*

Nope. As stated above, we get about 20% of our daily fluid needs met through the food we eat. That's because foods have their own fluid amounts and some, like fruits and vegetables, are over 90% water! Also, although water may be preferable for many reasons, just about any beverage can contribute toward your fluid intake for the day – milk, juice, even beer and coffee, though those come with their own considerations.

If it's starting to seem complicated, don't worry. Honestly, the reason the eight glasses a day rule became popular, in my opinion, is that it's easy to remember! There may not be any scientific evidence for this specific recommendation, but it's reasonable and memorable. The final option is to simply drink enough fluid so you don't feel thirsty and you produce light yellow urine.

*Can you drink too much water?*

Although rare, absolutely. Certain high intensity athletes, like marathon runners, are at greatest risk of overdoing it on the water, which can result in hyponatremia. Basically, the kidneys can't process the amount of water consumed, resulting in an electrolyte imbalance and low sodium levels in the blood. But, I wouldn't worry about this too much!

## Practice Exercise – Water Consumption

Review the liquids consumed in your food diaries and alcohol log. For each day:

- How much did you drink?
- Did you have symptoms of dehydration?

## Helpful Hints

- An easy way to drink extra water is to have a glass with and in between every meal.
- Drink a glass before, during, and after physical activity.
- Substitute water for alcohol when socializing.

If you do the above, I can virtually guarantee you will remain properly hydrated.

## Vignette

Maria came to me seeking assistance with her diet. First we clarified her overall goal. Did she want improved health, weight loss, or something different? Although not obese, Maria had struggled to lose the weight gained from her two previous pregnancies, the last of which was five years prior. She was concerned now however because her doctor informed her she was pre-diabetic – not quite there, but on the cusp of developing Type 2 Diabetes. That frightened Maria and she wanted to take proactive steps to reduce, or even eliminate, her risk. An admitted "candy addict", Maria explained that this was her biggest food vice.

Maria was 5'4" 150 lbs at the time we first met. These figures confirmed she was overweight and at risk for developing not just diabetes, but heart disease as well. Together we determined a weight of 130 lbs would be a reasonable goal. In addition, we would work on reducing her tendency to frequently overeat candy. In discussing the many different types of dietary lifestyles available to her, Maria felt it would work best within her traditional Southern family to not try anything too radical and simply work on developing an overall balanced diet, focusing on modifying what and how much she ate.

<u>Food diary</u>. The first step for Maria was to keep a food diary for two weeks so that we could both see exactly what she was eating – or

not eating, as the case turned out to be. Her diet was truly falling short in her tiny consumption of fruits and vegetables. The biggest additional issues with her food choices were her out of control portion sizes and her quite accurately described tendency to eat candy all day. Maria was also surprised to see just how little water or other fluid she was drinking each day.

<u>Meal planning</u>. Maria expressed a desire to make meal modifications for herself that would not negatively impact her husband or children. We decided to increase her water consumption first, both to improve her hydration and to help her learn to better distinguish when she was truly hungry. My recommendation was a glass of water with and between each meal, which Maria felt she would be able to ease into by adding one glass of water each day. We then focused on adding in fruits and vegetables with regard to modifying meal planning. The easiest way to do this was to include a piece of fruit or a vegetable (or a glass of 100% fruit/vegetable juice) at every meal.

<u>Portion control</u>. Since Maria was matching her portion sizes to her 6' 220 lbs husband, it was no wonder she was having trouble shedding pounds! I reviewed portion sizes with her and worked with her on understanding what portion size means when it's listed on a label. Slowly decreasing her calories, she essentially cut the amount of food she was eating in half and quickly realized she didn't even miss the extra.

<u>Candy</u>. Maria's toughest obstacle was reducing her candy consumption. We worked on this slowly, since the thought of going cold turkey was entirely unappealing for her. We set weekly reduction goals, with an ultimate goal of having one piece of candy per day. Together we identified substitute activities and distractions, like chewing gum, going for a walk, or drinking a glass of water, whenever she wanted to eat additional candy.

<u>Results</u>. There were setbacks along the way, of course. On days when Maria felt particularly stressed, she initially increased her food

(and especially candy) consumption. Using techniques like taking a bubble bath and doing low-impact aerobics helped her to increase her relaxation and she made steady improvement. By taking a reasonable and sustainable approach of losing one pound per week, and with a couple of setbacks, Maria attained her goal weight in 23 weeks, reduced her candy consumption to once per day, improved her fruit and vegetable consumption rate, and, most importantly, her doctor declared she was no longer pre-diabetic!

## Chapter Purpose

The purpose of this chapter is to start you thinking about what you put in your body, and whether it is consistent with your beliefs, the most helpful and healthful option, and ultimately sustainable over the long term. This chapter will be the beginning of your food journey; take time to review the practice exercises presented in this chapter to help you find your path:

## Practice Exercise Checklist

- Food Diary – If you want to effectively evaluate your eating patterns, you start with a basic log of every time you eat or drink anything for two weeks.

- Nutrient Needs – Once you have your Food Diary, you can evaluate it to determine if your nutrient needs are being met for optimal functioning by reviewing whether or not each day's meals and snacks include a protein, grain, and fruit/vegetable.

- Planning Your Meals – Identifying recipes through cookbooks or online sources, you can then plan your week's meals/snacks, grocery shop with the list of needed ingredients, and experiment with at least one new recipe each week.

- Dietary Lifestyle – Determining whether or not what you're eating reflects who you are and what you want to accomplish with your diet may necessitate moving in the direction of a more specific dietary lifestyle choice, such as becoming a vegetarian or going gluten-free.

- (Optional) Elimination Diet – Many people have allergies or food sensitivities. If you've noticed you simply don't feel well, try a simple elimination diet of cutting out one food item for 2-4 weeks, or a more complex elimination diet of cutting out gluten, dairy, sugar, and alcohol for 2-4 weeks, and based on how you feel, you can either stop there, or add items back in one at a time to see where the sensitivities may be.

- Uncovering Emotional Eating – Repeat the Food Diary exercise for two weeks, additionally noting thoughts and feelings when eating or drinking, including whether or not you are actually hungry, and then making the recommended immediate, short, and long term changes noted in the chapter.

- Alcohol Consumption (if you drink at all) – Track your alcohol consumption for two weeks, specifically noting where you are drinking; what your feelings are before, during, and after you drink; and how you feel physically immediately after consumption and the next day. Did your alcohol consumption result in positive or negative emotional and physical feelings?

- Water Consumption – Determine whether you are staying adequately hydrated by reviewing the liquid consumption noted in your Food and Alcohol Diaries, and whether you felt any of the symptoms of dehydration. If so, you can follow up with the Helpful Hints described.

Now that hopefully you're eating and feeling healthier, the natural follow up is physical activity. Continue with dietary changes as necessary or desired, even as you move forward in the program to the next *Step*.

# STEP 2
# PHYSICAL ACTIVITY

*I exercise today because it improves my quality of life.*
Tony Horton (Fitness instructor/creator of P90X)

Most people agree on physical activity in principle, but not always in practice. So, let's start with the principle. Physical activity, whether taking the stairs instead of the elevator or tying on the running shoes to do a couple of miles, is critically important to your wellbeing. Why? The short answer is…because. Our bodies were designed to be active. Most people (if they don't have a physical illness) will acknowledge they just feel better when they've been moderately physically active than when they haven't. Think about it historically, or evolutionarily. We used to have to hunt down our food…track it, stalk it, and finally kill it. All of that involved physical activity. It wasn't until we domesticated ourselves and then developed technological advances that allowed us to be completely sedentary for both work and play that we began struggling with this idea of physical activity.

Okay, so we seem to possibly have developed to be physically active. What are the benefits of increasing your physical activity now, when you clearly don't have to? The obvious benefit is your health. I leave it to you to do research into how exercise has health benefits. Suffice it to say, anecdotally with my own patients, I've seen people reduce or eliminate medication for diabetes, high blood pressure, and high cholesterol, just to name a few, by making dietary and physical activity changes.

Based also on personal and anecdotal experience, if you're more active, especially if you engage in focused deliberate exercise, you will naturally increase your fitness level. We'll get into specifics later, but if you vary your exercise to include activities like walking/running, weights/strength training, and dancing/Pilates, you can make the broadest impact on your fitness level. This translates into improved endurance, meaning you can run, bike, and swim farther and longer; improved muscle strength; and improved flexibility, likely meaning you can touch your toes and stand up straighter.

The premise of this entire book is that body, mind, and spirit are interconnected, and health in one area naturally leads to improved health in the others. How does this apply to physical activity? When physically active, people report their overall feeling of wellbeing increases, especially their self-esteem. You just feel better about yourself. In addition, research has consistently shown that exercise is one of the best ways to reduce symptoms of depression and anxiety. Isn't that great? You have complete control over how physically active you are, and thus can directly influence your mood.

This hopefully sounds promising – increasing physical activity will make you feel better in body, mind, and spirit.

*How much do you need to exercise?*

Hmm, this is the one that gets a little sticky and somewhat depends on who you ask. Across the board, the minimum recommendation has been 30 minutes of moderate physical activity preferably daily. What does that mean exactly? Any physical activity that quickens the breath and heart rate (e.g., a brisk walk).

Unfortunately, with today's hectic schedules, it can seem difficult if not impossible to find even 30 minutes in a day for physical activity. So, now a mini-lecture: everyone has the same 24 hours per day to work with. If you want to increase your physical activity, you need to prioritize it. Saying, "I don't have time", is just an excuse when you've chosen not to prioritize exercise. If you truly want to do it, you will. Okay, mini-lecture over.

The good news is you don't have to engage in your physical activity all at once. No matter how you break it up, when you're active, you're still utilizing your body in a healthful way. In other words, just because it doesn't take much time doesn't mean you don't derive benefit from, for example, parking a little further away from your destination and walking.

*Safety Caveat*

You know how when you see an advertisement on television for a new weight loss program or exercise regime, there's always that part about checking with your doctor before beginning this or any other program? Well, here goes my legal disclaimer. I'm about to get into specifics about incorporating physical activity into your daily life. For most people, you probably won't need to consult with your healthcare provider first. However, if you're middle-aged, have a health condition, or anticipate increasing your exercise level significantly, it would probably be best to check with your doc first. And remember, I'm not a medical doctor. Thanks.

## Identifying an Acceptable Weight

One of the trickiest things to determine is what's considered a healthy weight for your height. People often have their own ideas – weighing what they did in high school; reaching a magical number on the scale; when they're able to wear a particularly sized article of clothing. Unfortunately, that may or may not be a true reflection of a healthy weight for your body size and shape. It's more than just comparing your weight to your height. But, that's where we'll start!

Everyone is probably familiar with the height-weight chart. It pictorially shows what's considered a healthy weight given a specific height. There are charts for children and adolescents, focusing more on developmental growth. There are charts for the military, focusing on what optimizes being fit to fight. There has been the general government chart, assisting citizens with identifying and, if necessary, rectifying their weight issues.

Clearly, there really isn't a standardized height-weight chart anymore. This makes sense because there are so many variables that are involved in determining if an individual is a healthy weight for their height. Is the individual male or female? Men typically are heavier than same-height females. How big- or small-boned is the person? If you have a larger frame, it may actually be unhealthy to match the weight of a smaller-boned person. How muscular is the person? Muscle is denser than fat, so simply looking at weight may not accurately capture the individual's level of health. Can you see why standardization would be challenging?

*So should you chuck the charts?*

Well, I wouldn't hold them up as infallible, but they can be helpful in getting a general sense of how your height compares to your ideal healthy weight. And, some charts do try to account for the issues identified above. For example, all charts have separate entries for males and females. Other charts even consider the overall size of the person's structure, as these for Females and Males, respectively, from the Metropolitan Life Insurance Company.

Females:

| Height | Small Frame | Medium Frame | Large Frame |
|---|---|---|---|
| 4'10" | 102-111 | 109-121 | 118-131 |
| 4'11" | 103-113 | 111-123 | 120-134 |
| 5'0" | 104-115 | 113-126 | 122-137 |

| Height | Small Frame | Medium Frame | Large Frame |
|---|---|---|---|
| 5'1" | 106-118 | 115-129 | 125-140 |
| 5'2" | 108-121 | 118-132 | 128-143 |
| 5'3" | 111-124 | 121-135 | 131-147 |
| 5'4" | 114-127 | 124-138 | 134-151 |
| 5'5" | 117-130 | 127-141 | 137-155 |
| 5'6" | 120-133 | 130-144 | 140-159 |
| 5'7" | 123-136 | 133-147 | 143-163 |
| 5'8" | 126-139 | 136-150 | 146-167 |
| 5'9" | 129-142 | 139-153 | 149-170 |
| 5'10" | 132-145 | 142-156 | 152-173 |
| 5'11" | 135-148 | 145-159 | 155-176 |
| 6'0" | 138-151 | 148-162 | 158-179 |

Males:

| Height | Small Frame | Medium Frame | Large Frame |
|---|---|---|---|
| 5'2" | 128-134 | 131-141 | 138-150 |
| 5'3" | 130-136 | 133-143 | 140-153 |
| 5'4" | 132-138 | 135-145 | 142-156 |
| 5'5" | 134-140 | 137-148 | 144-160 |
| 5'6" | 136-142 | 139-151 | 141-164 |
| 5'7" | 138-145 | 142-154 | 149-168 |
| 5'8" | 140-148 | 145-157 | 152-172 |
| 5'9" | 142-151 | 148-160 | 155-171 |

| 5'10" | 144-154 | 151-163 | 158-180 |
| --- | --- | --- | --- |
| 5'11" | 146-157 | 154-166 | 161-184 |
| 6'0" | 149-160 | 157-170 | 164-188 |
| 6'1" | 152-164 | 160-174 | 168-192 |
| 6'2" | 155-168 | 164-178 | 172-197 |
| 6'3" | 158-172 | 167-182 | 176-202 |
| 6'4" | 162-176 | 171-187 | 181-207 |

*What's next after the charts?*

To appropriately consider the amount of bone, muscle, and fat in your body's composition, you want to determine your body mass index. Bone and muscle are obviously important, but measuring the amount of body fat is the critical piece in determining just how healthy or not your current weight can be considered.

Direct measures of body fat include underwater weighing (pretty much exactly what it sounds like), bioelectrical impedance (passing an electric current through the body to measure fat), and dual energy x-ray absorptiometry (just about as complicated and expensive as it sounds). Luckily, there is an alternative that, while not measuring fat directly, has been shown to correlate well to such direct measures. This alternative is the body mass index, or BMI.

BMI is calculated from your weight and height; it's standardized, meaning it's the same for males and females. It's easy to calculate and thus is a great, inexpensive way to identify folks who might have a weight problem. Why do I say might? For my astute readers, you may have already identified the problem, since it is the same as with the height-weight charts. Bigger-boned or muscular individuals will likely end up with a higher BMI, suggesting a higher percentage of body fat that is not accurate. Thus, although a person may be considered overweight according to the BMI categories (discussed below), they still may not be. Nevertheless, statistically, BMI is a fairly good indicator of body fatness, overweight, and obesity.

## Practice Exercise – Determining Healthy Weight

There are concrete steps you can take that will give you a pretty good idea of whether or not your weight is healthy for you.

1. Use the above charts:
   Height      _____
   Weight      _____
   Frame size  _____

   Where are you on the above male or female chart?
   What range?
   Are you above, below, or within the suggested weight for your height, gender, and frame size?

2. Calculate your BMI easily with a calculator and the below formula (or go to any of the myriad websites online that simply ask you to input your height and weight, then spit out a number):

Calculate your BMI by dividing your weight in pounds by your height in inches squared and then multiplying the result by a conversion factor of 703.

For a visual aid: Formula: weight (lb) / [height (in)]$^2$ x 703

And an example: Weight = 130 lbs; Height = 5'4" (64 in)

Calculation: $130 / (64)^2 \times 703 = 22.3$

Now you'll want to find your number in the table below (websites that offer BMI calculators will also include an interpretation and standard BMI table):

| BMI | Weight Status |
|---|---|
| Below 18.5 | Underweight |
| 18.5 – 24.9 | Normal |
| 25.0 – 29.9 | Overweight |
| 30.0 and Above | Obese |

So, for our example BMI above, our 5'4" 130 pound individual with a BMI of 22 is solidly within the Normal range and thus, most likely is a perfectly healthy weight for her height.

Note: BMI is calculated the same for children and adults, but I am going to forego interpreting for children at this point. If you have concerns about your child being underweight or overweight, consult with your healthcare provider. And remember, for adults, BMI is the same for men and women of all ages.

3. There is an additional inexpensive assessment, known as the skinfold thickness measurement or caliper test, that can assist in determining percentage of body fat. This too has a caveat – the skill of the individual utilizing the caliper to measure the fold of skin being the predominant one. In my experience, the easiest way to check this one is at a gym. But, if you've done steps 1 and 2 above, you probably don't need it.

Use your own sense of comfort in your skin, along with the charts and BMI, to help you determine if you need to gain, maintain, or lose weight.

You might be wondering, given all this talk about healthy weight for a specific height, if there's any guidance for how often a person ought to check to see how their weight is doing. There are natural fluctuations in weight throughout the day, and even throughout the week, based on many factors. Bottom line, if you're concerned about your weight, weighing once a week is likely optimal for monitoring your status, without risking becoming obsessive over the exact number on the scale. The ideal way to track this is to weigh yourself first thing in the morning, on the same day of the week, completely naked. This way, you can account for many of the natural fluctuations.

## Exercise!

Hopefully, I've convinced you that physical activity is an important part of everyday life. For most people, this means some form of exercise. Let's figure out what could make it important in your life, if it isn't already.

## Practice Exercise – Fitness Goals

What are your fitness goals? Writing them down will help you clarify your specific hopes and desires; several examples are listed for you:

1. E.g., Change weight
2. Gain muscle
3. _____
4. _____
5. _____

In my experience, men tend to focus on weight lifting for strength, women on cardio for weight loss, and a few of both occasionally do something to improve flexibility. However, and I think you know what I'm going to say next, you really need a little bit of all three to optimize your physical fitness.

*Cardiovascular Fitness*

Exercise to improve cardiovascular functioning is what we call aerobic exercise (not to be confused with the type of exercise known as aerobics, of course). Many people immediately picture running indefinitely on a treadmill when they think about doing aerobic exercise. Certainly that is a very reasonable option. But, it's also very limiting. At the gym, one can obviously use the treadmill (and I actually am quite a fan), but there are many other options, including the elliptical, Stairmaster, rowing machine, and stationary bicycle. Also, depending on the facilities you are using, there are classes you can take, such as step class, Zumba, and spinning. If the thought of exercising indoors makes you automatically yawn, move your activity to the outdoors.

Outdoor exercise is wonderful because you can enjoy the beauty of nature (even in a city) while feeling more a part of your community. Depending on the season, you may have a variety of activities to choose from. In the warmer months, you can walk, jog, run, cycle, play soccer, or inline skate. Many cities have clubs where you can engage in the activities with other like-minded individuals. Getting up to cycle 20 miles on a Saturday morning might be easier if you know there's a group of people waiting for you in the park! In the colder months, depending on your comfort level, you can engage in the above activities, but you can also try others, such as ice skating or cross country skiing.

Naturally, many sports can be played indoors or out, such as basketball, swimming, and racquetball. You can also try to find a local team – or maybe get together with folks you work with – to add that interpersonal touch to your exercise. Generally, you want to engage in aerobic exercise 3-4 times per week; though honestly, if you can do at least thirty minutes every day, that would be preferable.

*Weight Training*

Men do it and women avoid it for the same reason – the belief that lifting weights will create larger, bulky muscles. Luckily, this is pretty much a myth for women. Men, yes, can bulk up by lifting weights. Women, not so much. Biologically, it takes a heck of a lot of effort (and testosterone!) for a woman to create bulky muscles. Weight lifting a couple of times a week simply isn't going to do it.

Depending on your fitness goals, the details of your weight training regimen will vary. A good rule of thumb initially is at least 20-30 minutes 2-3 times per week. You can join a gym for access to the weights and weight machines, or you can buy a set of hand weights, dumbbells, or kettlebells, and download sample exercise programs off the Internet. For example, in our home gym, my husband and I have a squat rack, barbells, weight bands, kettlebells, and dumbbells/free weights in increments from 3lbs up to 45 lbs for use with routines we've found online. A few websites that offer assistance in creating a weight lifting plan include shape.com, muscleandfitness.com, and bodybuilding.com.

*Flexibility Training*

Flexibility is the oft forgotten piece of exercise, yet it can make all the other components more effective – in addition, who doesn't want to have the ability to touch their toes? The most the average exerciser may do is stretch before and/or after working out. But, it can be of benefit to engage in a longer bit of flexibility training.

Flexibility is, by definition, the ability of a joint to move through its full range of motion. And, although certain individuals, like dancers, could probably fairly accurately be described as "flexible" for the most part, people have varying degrees of flexibility within their own bodies.

The easiest ways to add flexibility can be to buy a couple of DVDs with some 20-30 minute routines on them. Yoga, Pilates, and classical dance (e.g., ballet) are all excellent choices. Some gyms also offer classes of variable intensity, duration, and skill level that may work out well for you. Finally, there are streaming fitness programs available as well. So you don't have to do yoga, but you may find it fun and healthful!

## Practice Exercise – Exercise Log

At this point, you will most benefit from truly tracking the amount of exercise you're getting. Just like with tracking food and drink, folks tend to over- or under-estimate what they're doing. It's best to track for two weeks to get accurate results! Track the following (the bottom half of this page has a fillable form to photocopy, if you prefer):

1. Date/time:
2. Activity:
    Cardio?
    Strength?
    Flexibility?
3. Length of time:
4. Intensity (1-10):

## Exercise Log

| Date/Time | Activity | Cardio (Y/N) | Strength (Y/N) | Flexibility (Y/N) | Length of time | Intensity (1-10) |
|---|---|---|---|---|---|---|
| | | | | | | |
| | | | | | | |
| | | | | | | |
| | | | | | | |
| | | | | | | |
| | | | | | | |
| | | | | | | |

After your two weeks, what do you see? Are you exercising at least three times per week? Are you doing a mix of activities? How is your intensity level? If you don't have variety, duration, and intensity, what can you add or otherwise do differently?

## Maintaining Motivation

If you're like most people, you start any exercise program with a ton of enthusiasm. You go through your day, excited about the steps you are taking to be healthier, lose weight, or whatever your specific goal may be. Then, as the days or weeks pass, as the number on the scale doesn't change, or your speed at the mile run doesn't improve, you find yourself flagging. Soon, when your alarm goes off for your morning run, you're hitting the snooze button; after work, you look at your workout clothes so carefully laid out that morning, and decide to just watch some television. Does this sound like you? What you need are lessons in motivation!

*How can you stay motivated?*
Motivation is probably the single biggest factor in determining success in reaching a goal or simply maintaining healthy choices. Boredom, stress, and lack of progress all work together to sabotage our efforts. Thankfully, there are ways to stay motivated. Overall, think of exercising as something you do for yourself, that helps you stay physically and emotionally balanced. And, when that isn't sufficiently motivating, try each of the methods below and you will find yourself remaining eager to continue exercising.

*Where can you start?*
Keeping an exercise journal or log (like you started above) is one of the best ways to both start exercising and maintain motivation to continue. Initially, keeping the journal will help you establish what you're doing and how often. As you move forward, however, the

exercise journal can accomplish so much more. In addition to noting what exercise you're doing and when, you may find it helpful to note the following as well in your log:

1. How do you feel immediately before and after exercising, as well as throughout your day?
2. Do you look forward to certain types of exercise or certain times of the day more than others?
3. Are you noting positive changes to your mood, energy level, quality of sleep, etc?

Bottom line, by tracking the impact of specific exercises, you can determine which ones benefit you personally the most and focus more on those. In addition, because your body adjusts to activity, I recommend changing your workout routine every three months.

*Do you need to schedule?*

Maybe it goes without saying, but I'm going to say it anyway – if you don't schedule your exercise, your mind is liable to interpret that as exercise not being important. Admit it, we schedule things that are important for us to do. If you really want to make sure you exercise daily, then put it in your planner. Many opinions exist about when the best time of day is to exercise – morning, afternoon, or evening. My opinion? The best time of day to exercise is whenever you believe you are more likely to do it! If you don't do it, then it doesn't matter if it was planned for the "best" time of day or not, now does it?

*How can you increase your likelihood of success?*

People can be highly creative when it comes to finding excuses not to exercise. One way to stay on track is to identify those potential excuses in advance and have a mental response to tell yourself for each one.

## Practice Exercise – Hurdling Excuses

If you're unsure what some of your excuses might be to not exercise, think about past attempts to develop and maintain an exercise routine. What excuses did you give yourself in times past? Note them below:

1. _____
2. _____
3. _____
4. _____
5. _____

## The key is to identify your primary excuses and have your counterarguments ready!

Let's look at common excuses and possible solutions.

1. An extremely common excuse is the time factor. When you find yourself thinking, "I just don't have time to exercise", remind yourself what I said earlier about how we all have the same 24 hours to work with in a day and consider how you can fit exercise in. Take simple steps, like preparing your workout clothes in advance or planning for shorter workouts.
2. Another somewhat common excuse is being overly sore from a prior workout, thus requiring taking time off. If this is you, prepare to bring your intensity down a notch or have a lower intensity workout ready to go for the next day, in case you aren't able to avoid muscle soreness.
3. One of the most effective ways to fight boredom and decreased motivation is to establish a workout routine with a bunch of variety. This is logical, right? If you're running every single time you do cardio, eventually that may wear on you. On the other hand, if you run one day, bike another, and swim for a third, the likelihood of staving off boredom

greatly increases. If you think of typical exercises and think, "ugh, if I have to bike one more time, I'm eating a pint of Ben & Jerry's", then try something more engaging that maybe is so fun, you won't even think of it as exercise. For example, if you like rhythmic movement, try taking a dance class, whether ballet, Latin, or belly. If you belong to a larger gym with more offerings, maybe you can try Pilates, Zumba, or kickboxing. When your motivation lags, try something new.

## Helpful Hints

As with anything in life, your eagerness to engage in exercise is likely going to fluctuate from day to day, week to week. What motivates one day may be completely useless the next. Work with your fluctuations as best you can and look for inspiration everywhere.

1. Try not to take more than one day off at time. I'm sure you know, the more time off you take, the easier it becomes to justify another day off. Before you give up, try anything and everything to remain focused and moving forward.
2. One way to ensure you at least do something each day is, when you find yourself reluctant to exercise, tell yourself you'll just do 10 minutes. Then, if you want to (and usually you will), you can finish the originally intended workout. And, if you don't want to continue, then clearly you needed a break, but you've still done those 10 minutes.
3. Finally, don't be so hard on yourself if you do miss a couple of workouts. The key is to get back on that horse, as they say. In other words, resume your exercise schedule as though you'd been maintaining all along. Trust me, you'll quickly feel more positive again.

*Are you wondering why you're not buff and beautiful already?*
Another lesson in reality. When you think back to times you

and/or your friends have not succeeded at fitness goals, how often has it been related to unrealistic goals? Yep, it's pretty common. Sometimes, we start off so excited and motivated to lose weight, rock weight lifter muscles, or fit into that sexy little black dress. Then the days, weeks, and maybe even months pass, and … nada. We look in the mirror and we don't see the fabulous body we were expecting when we started. Becoming physically fit is a process and it's important to maintain realistic expectations about how fast you will progress, keeping in mind you may even take a few steps back along the way. If you develop realistic goals and give yourself time to accomplish them, while allowing for slip ups and backward movement, you will find yourself more easily remaining on track.

*How exactly do goals fit in?*

Think of what you identified at the beginning of this section as your fitness goals. Likely they were fairly general, like lose weight or gain muscle. Our next step then will be to identify more specific goals, either within your more general goals, or something you've just always been interested in. This can range from a beginning goal, like walking around the neighborhood, to more substantial goals, such as running a 5K, a marathon, or even a triathlon.

## Practice Exercise – Identifying Specific Goals

Have you always wanted to accomplish some significant personal physical goal? Go all the way back to childhood if you need to:

1. E.g., Run a marathon
2. Learn to tango
3. _____
4. _____
5. _____

Can you visualize yourself crossing the finish line of...whatever you've always wanted to do? Seize that interest and develop a goal to motivate yourself. Go online and find workout plans for accomplishing your goal. Place the plan on your refrigerator so you will consistently have that visual reminder that, yes, you have a goal.

Don't forget to reward yourself. Rewarding yourself for maintaining your exercise regime can run the gamut from a simple visual reminder (such as just mentioned above) to a lavish vacation. You'd be amazed how motivating a simple checkbox on the calendar for every day's completed workout can be. Every time you look at the calendar, you'll think, "Yes!, I did that".

## Practice Exercise – Identifying Rewards

Now that you've identified more specific goals, work to attach them to short- and long-term rewards (a little bigger, more expensive, or involved) for reaching those goals:

| Short-Term Rewards | Long-Term Rewards |
|---|---|
| 1. E.g., Movie | Climbing equipment |
| 2. Massage | Weekend getaway |
| 3. Running magazine subscription | Cruise |
| 4. _____ | _____ |
| 5. _____ | _____ |
| 6. _____ | _____ |

Note: If you can relate your reward to fitness, even better!

Oh, but try to avoid rewarding yourself with food! If your goal is improved health or weight loss, then clearly a food reward might be counterproductive.

*One is a lonely number*

An extremely effective method to stay motivated is to be accountable to someone else. In other words, exercise with a buddy, whether a single other person, a group, or a more organized team. You can join an informal neighborhood cycling group. Or you can look for a community soccer team. Or you can even join a marathon training group. Keep in mind, too, that this doesn't even have to be in person. You can join an online community that will offer encouragement and support to log and track your daily exercising. Simply go to a search engine and type in your activity, or even simply "weight loss", and a plethora of options will materialize. You can also check out various Facebook groups and Meetup.com groups. Review your options and go with what seems like a good fit.

*What about benefiting others?*

One way to combine all of the above is to adopt a goal that pushes you, involves working with others, and ultimately benefits an organization that could use support. In other words, combine your exercising with charity fundraising. Volunteering to fundraise for a worthy organization as part of an exercise goal will help you stay on track, as well as give you warm fuzzies. There are many organizations that hold walk/run/bike/dance events to raise awareness and money. Some of the ones I've participated with in the past include the American Cancer Society's Relay For Life, the Court-Appointed Special Advocates, and the National Association for the Mentally Ill. I've also done 5K walks for animal welfare and to end domestic abuse. Many of these organizations will provide training, especially for substantial and difficult distances.

*Do you work best alone?*

If you are one of those individuals who prefers to work out on a solitary basis, that's okay. The key to maintaining motivation when you're working out solo is to make sure there's something fun to occupy your mind. Some folks just zone out when running or cycling, and that's cool, but many people find their motivation dipping as their minds wander. An obvious answer is putting together a great, variable-speed music playlist. This can bring you from warm up through cool down with nary a desire to stop. Google "exercise song playlist" and I guarantee you'll find more options than you'll know what to do with! If you want something a little different, try an audio book. Just make sure that you don't get so swept up in the story that you find yourself lost or trip over an object in your path.

*Think about why you're doing this*

The final motivator I want to comment on is excitement. Remember how you felt when you first began your exercise routine? You were undoubtedly super excited and felt fully confident that this time, things would be different and you would be successful. Flash forward a few weeks or even months…my how things have changed! Hopefully, all of the above motivation suggestions will be helpful to you, but I leave you with this final one. Regain some of that initial excitement by remembering why exactly you started down this path. Was it to lose weight, gain muscle, lower your diabetes risk, complete a marathon, or raise $1000 for the American Cancer Society? Remind yourself of why you wanted to exercise and maybe you can recapture some of that initial excitement.

## "I Hate Exercising!"

Oh, the lamentation… Many people seem to have an intractable problem with engaging in "exercise", though hopefully, in the discussion above, you've seen that exercising can contain tremendous variety and satisfaction. If that didn't do the trick, however, I can let you in on a little secret (though maybe it's not such a little secret by now) – any physical activity will work. You don't, strictly speaking, have to engage in exercise to derive the benefits of exercise.

*What can you do instead?*

Since any physical activity will work, the possibilities are endless.

To start, think about ways you already engage in physical activity:
- Unless you've hired someone to do it for you, you likely clean your house; this involves vacuuming, mopping, and dusting that engages muscles, and depending on how fast you go and how many breaks you take, can be a cardio workout.
- Outside, every time you wash and/or wax your car, you're engaging in physical activity.
- Or how about all that time you spend in the garden? Weeding, raking, planting, mowing – all of these are physical activities.
- As a final example, consider when you go clothes and grocery shopping. Walking around the mall and pushing a grocery cart are two more examples of physical activity in your everyday life that you are likely already doing.

## Practice Exercise – Non-Exercise Physical Activity

What non-exercise physical activity do you already engage in?
1. _____
2. _____
3. _____
4. _____

## Helpful Hint

If you really want to know how much non-exercise physical activity you engage in, more than just filling out the above, you can keep a physical activity log, similar to the other logs you've done, and track exactly what you're doing each and every day that gets your blood pumping.

Obviously, even with all you do every day, there's more that can be done to increase your physical activity level closer to what's recommended for daily activity. Taking the examples from above, let's see how we can increase our physical activity level:

- Park in the farthest parking spot possible in the lot and increase your amount of walking.
- Carry a basket instead of pushing a cart at the store if it's only for a few items.
- Ditch the mechanical equipment when gardening and instead use, for example, a hand mower rather than a power mower.

Beyond increasing the physical engagement of activities you already do, there are multiple opportunities throughout your day to simply add in physical activity:

- Take every opportunity to use the stairs instead of the elevator.
- Ditch your car. Cycle or walk to nearby friends' homes or shopping centers.
- When sitting at your desk at work, use an exercise ball instead of a chair, and/or engage in calisthenics and simple stretches; e.g., I do 20 jumping jacks after every hour-long treatment session at work.

The key with all of these suggestions is to keep in the back of your mind the idea that you want to engage in as much natural physical activity as you can. Making basic changes or additions to activities you already do can be one of the easiest ways to increase your overall physical activity.

Since for many people one of the reasons to increase physical activity is for weight loss, I thought it would be helpful to include a physical activity chart for both exercising and everyday activities.

Thanks to the American College of Sports Medicine for publishing the below chart online:

Calories Expended During Specific Activities

| ACTIVITY* | Calories expended in 30 minutes Male (175 lbs) | Calories expended in 30 minutes Female (135 lbs) |
|---|---|---|
| Biking 12-13.9 mph (moderate effort) | 334 | 258 |
| Circuit Training | 334 | 258 |
| Stretching, hatha yoga | 167 | 129 |
| Dancing - general | 188 | 145 |
| Dancing - ballet, modern | 251 | 193 |
| House Cleaning - vigorous (mop, wash car) | 188 | 145 |
| House Cleaning - light (dusting, vacuuming) | 104 | 81 |
| Playing w/ kids moderate - walk/run | 167 | 129 |
| Gardening | 209 | 161 |
| Mowing lawn - Hand mower | 251 | 193 |
| Running - 6 mph | 418 | 322 |
| Jogging | 292 | 225 |
| Basketball - Game | 334 | 258 |
| Children's Games | 209 | 161 |
| Football | 334 | 258 |
| Frisbee | 125 | 97 |
| Horseback Riding | 167 | 129 |
| Skating | 292 | 225 |
| Soccer | 292 | 225 |
| Softball/Baseball | 209 | 161 |
| Tennis | 292 | 225 |

| Hiking | 251 | 193 |
| --- | --- | --- |
| Walking - 4 mph, level surface | 167 | 129 |
| Walking - leisure | 146 | 113 |
| Canoeing/Rowing - moderate | 292 | 225 |
| Kayaking | 209 | 161 |
| Swimming laps freestyle - moderate | 334 | 258 |

\* Data from *ACSM Resource Manual for Guidelines for Exercise Testing and Prescription Third Edition*

## Vignette

Elle struggled with maintaining a regular exercise routine. In college, she had been on the track team. Since graduating, marrying, and having a child, she found it increasingly difficult to make the time to exercise. When she did exercise, she quickly became bored. I started off working with Elle by helping her determine what her fitness goals were – and it turned out she really didn't have any! Clearly that was the first problem, so that's where we started.

Through the use of Socratic questioning, Elle considered all of the reasons she had exercised before and why she wanted to do so again. Due to her former athletic life, she was the weight she wanted, but she didn't have the muscle tone she had once upon a time. In addition, she missed the camaraderie of being on a sports team and missed having a fitness purpose. Taking all of this into consideration, I worked with Elle on creating an exercise routine that would energize and motivate her.

<u>Muscle tone</u>. Elle already had a membership at the local YMCA, so the first thing we tackled was the missing muscle tone. Elle went by the gym and met with an onsite trainer who developed an overall strength training program specific to her needs, working her entire

body, but focusing on her legs. She agreed to strength train two times per week for 30 minutes, plus one day for taking a yoga class. In reviewing her schedule, it became apparent that she had time after work for this training. She tacked up a picture of herself from her college days, to assist with maintaining motivation to strength train, never her favorite part of exercising.

Fitness purpose. Since Elle previously ran track, she was accustomed to competition and following a running schedule. Elle had never done long-distance running before, but with questioning she identified that this was something she had always wanted to try. Therefore, she located a half-marathon taking place in two months and a new goal was born! Because of her natural ability and running history, together we developed a training program that would prepare her for race day. This 8 week program consisted of running four days per week, cross training on a fifth, and taking two days for rest. The running distances and intensities gradually increased as she moved through the program (if this sounds like something you'd like to try, simply Google "half-marathon training" or find a smart phone app; I personally use the free MapMyRun Trainer by MapMyFitness). Finding the time required some creativity and shifting of responsibilities in her schedule, but Elle's excitement to start a training program motivated her to do whatever was necessary.

Camaraderie. Nearly all towns and cities have running clubs, and Elle's town was no different. To regain that sense of being part of a team that Elle missed from her college days, she sought out and joined her local running club. Running with club members fulfilled that missing sense of fun, and also provided her ample opportunity to push herself by running with faster or more enduring runners. Elle found her times improving by leaps and bounds, simply by having others to compete with in a no-stress way.

Two months after we developed this plan, Elle successfully completed her first half-marathon with an established personal best that she has already declared she will beat at her next half-marathon!

In addition, she has made many new friends and feels healthier physically and mentally. She anticipates easily continuing to stay inspired by remembering what explicitly motivates her, like establishing specific goals, and ensuring she continues to do that.

## Chapter Purpose

The purpose of this chapter is to start you down a path of physical health, with both exercise and everyday activity. I asked you many questions about your fitness goals, how much you are or are not exercising, developing plans for modifying and/or increasing your physical activity, and how to maintain motivation by making a commitment to physical activity. This chapter will be the beginning of your physical activity journey; take time to review the practice exercises presented in this chapter to help you find your path:

## Practice Exercise Checklist

- Determining Healthy Weight – One of the best places to start is with determining whether or not you are at a healthy body weight; this practice exercise offers the height/weight chart, calculating BMI, and skinfold thickness measurement as options.

- Fitness Goals – By writing down what your fitness goals are, which may be quite general at this stage, it helps to clarify your hopes and desires moving forward.

- Exercise Log – If you want to effectively determine and evaluate your exercise patterns, start with a basic log of every time you exercise for two weeks, noting activity (cardio, strength, and/or flexibility), length of time, and intensity.

- Hurdling Excuses – It can become quite easy to rationalize skipping a workout; the first step in overcoming excuses is to identify them, which this practice exercise encourages you to do, before offering solutions.

- Identifying Specific Goals – "Lose weight" may be a common goal, but it is also too general. Staying focused and motivated is easier with more specific goals, e.g., lose one pound per week.

- Identifying Rewards – Maintaining motivation can be helped by rewarding ourselves for meeting short- and long-term exercise goals, especially if we can tie the reward into physical activity, e.g., new workout gear for attending six months of yoga classes.

- Non-Exercise Physical Activity – Exercise is a dirty word for some people so it's important to identify the physical activity we do on a daily basis, whether through housework, yard work, grocery shopping, walking through parking lots, etc.

Physical activity is a critical component to happiness because our bodies truly were designed to move. This may involve dedicated exercising or it may involve simply making more active choices, or both. But, none of that matters if you're tired and restless.

DR. HEATHER SILVIO

# STEP 3
# SLEEP & MEDITATION

*Sleep is the best meditation.*
Dalai Lama (Spiritual leader of the Tibetan people)

This final step under the *Body* section consists of two areas related to rejuvenation: sleep and meditation. Without adequate sleep, everything else suffers. I'm sure you've noticed crabbiness in yourself and others when you are tired. How about decreased concentration, increased appetite, and duller skin? The fact is that sleep is critical to our basic functioning and therefore intimately connected to our life's satisfaction. I also include meditation in this section because rejuvenation is about much more than just quality sleep. Sometimes, we may want to quiet and refocus our minds, but without actually sleeping. Meditation offers that opportunity.

## To Sleep Perchance to Dream

Sleep. We all know what it is and that we need it. We know it's unpleasant when elusive and refreshing when obtained. But, what is it and why is it so important? Let's start off with some basic information about the sleep cycle and what sleep does for the body.

Without getting too technical, there are two primary types of sleep – rapid eye movement (REM) and non-rapid eye movement

(NREM) sleep. NREM accounts for up to 75% of the time spent asleep, and although there is relatively little dreaming, it is during a stage of this type of sleep that you are most likely to experience events like night terrors or sleep walking. REM accounts for the other 25% of our time spent asleep and is where we experience dreaming.

There are many theories, but no conclusions, regarding the purpose sleep serves. Some of these theories include restoration of the body, support of body and brain development, and the processing of memories. Although we do not know with certainty why we need to sleep, we just know we need to.

*What can happen without enough quality sleep?*

Sleep deprivation can negatively impact both physical and mental/emotional functioning:

- Physical impacts:
    - Fatigue.
    - Appetite increase.
    - Headaches.
    - Diabetes.
    - Weight gain and obesity.
    - Cardiovascular disease.
    - Immune system issues, resulting in frequent infections.
    - Impaired motor skills and increased risk of accidents.
- Mental/Emotional impacts:
    - Confusion and concentration problems.
    - Irritability.
    - Lack of motivation.
    - Depression.
    - Moodiness.
    - Reduced creativity.
    - Reduced problem solving skills.
    - Inability to cope with stress.

*How much sleep do you need?*

The National Sleep Foundation has made specific recommendations, based on age, for how much sleep people need. We need the most amount of sleep as infants, with the amount decreasing as we age. Adolescents, ages 10-17, need about 8.5-9.5 hours and adults need 7-9 hours. How many of you actually get that amount consistently, if not every day?

## Practice Exercise – Sleep Diary

How much sleep do you get? This exercise asks you to keep a sleep diary for two weeks, estimating* the following:

|           | Fell Asleep | Woke Up | Add'l Times |
|-----------|-------------|---------|-------------|
| Monday    |             |         |             |
| Tuesday   |             |         |             |
| Wednesday |             |         |             |
| Thursday  |             |         |             |
| Friday    |             |         |             |
| Saturday  |             |         |             |
| Sunday    |             |         |             |

*Estimates only because I don't want you staring at the clock!

Note that the diary asks you to track when you believe you fell asleep, when you woke up, if you had additional night wakings, and/or if you took naps during the day.

*How do you feel after each day?*
Consider the connection between how you feel and how much sleep you got each of the nights. Bottom line, get enough sleep to feel rested and restored in the morning!

*If it were that easy, you would, right?*

Ah yes, the industrial-age old complaint. There aren't enough hours in the day to get the recommended amount of sleep. Or, sleep is difficult due to problems falling or staying asleep, or both. Luckily, there are basic recommendations to assist in all these areas. This next section will discuss things you can do for yourself and within your environment to improve the quantity and quality of your sleep.

Controlling your environment, modifying your personal behaviors, and engaging in relaxation exercises will very likely improve the quantity and quality of your sleep. How do these do that? When we begin experiencing sleep difficulty, most people make intuitive decisions that, unfortunately, are counterproductive. What these recommendations will do is help to break the bad habits and mental associations that interfere with sleep. I am basically going to help you rewire your brain!

1. The first step is to go to bed only when you're sleepy. This might seem obvious, but I cannot tell you how many people go to bed when they think they "should" figuring they'll eventually fall asleep, and that at least while they're laying there, they're getting some rest. Wrong! Going to bed before you're sleepy does nothing but cause your mind to associate the bed with being awake. That clearly isn't helpful. If you aren't tired, don't try to sleep.

2. If you don't fall asleep within a reasonable time frame (15-20 minutes), then get back out of bed until you are sleepy. The key is to do something boring and non-activating, like reading a technical manual; if you get out of bed and do something activating, like watching an action movie, you're not helping yourself. Just as noted above, staying in bed for sometimes hours until you fall asleep simply results in your mind associating being in bed with being awake.

3. Using the bed for sleep and sex only will assist your mind in associating the bed with being asleep. Many people like to watch television, play on the laptop, read a book, or listen to music while in bed. Until you've achieved the sleep pattern you desire, all of those activities are forbidden in the bedroom. The best option might be to completely remove all of these possible distractions from the bedroom, so they aren't even available as temptations or visual reminders.

4. One thing people don't often think about is the physical environment of their bedroom. Is it too light or too dark? How about too cold or too hot? Are there random noises or is it too quiet? When you have trouble falling asleep, or when you wake up during the night, take note if there is any physical discomfort. If the light coming in from a streetlight is distracting, you may consider a sleep mask. If you've kicked off your covers and you still feel like you're on fire, you may need to adjust the thermostat or turn on the fan.

5. Going to bed at the same time every night and rising at the same time every morning will assist you in improving your sleep. Similar to not staying in bed when you can't sleep, by maintaining the same sleep schedule you will train your brain to expect to sleep and rise at specific times. I realize that folks typically like to sleep in on the weekends. That's okay to a limited extent. An unofficial rule of thumb that has worked with my patients is to not sleep later than two hours on the weekends than you do during the week.

6. Certain substances can negatively impact your sleep: alcohol, nicotine, and caffeine. Although alcohol has a reputation for helping people fall asleep, even if it is able to do that, many people report fractured sleep and wake not rested. Nicotine,

as a stimulant, activates the body and will interfere with sleep; avoid smoking or dipping within a couple of hours of bedtime if possible. And, finally caffeine. Many people might be surprised to learn that it can take up to eight hours for caffeine to leave the body. Therefore, if you ingest it, do so no later than lunchtime, so you can be absolutely sure it isn't interfering with your sleep.

7. As discussed in earlier sections, healthy eating and consistent exercise are critical to physical and emotional wellbeing. However, if you engage in either of these activities too close to bedtime, your sleep may be negatively impacted. Exercise is clearly activating of the body and mind; therefore, you really want to make sure you do it at least two hours before you go to bed. With food, you don't want to go to bed hungry (because your body will start looking for food and keep you awake) or full (because then your body will be focused on digesting what you ate). Aim for eating something relatively light within a couple of hours of bedtime.

*What if you still can't sleep*

Many people report that when they try to go to sleep, they may feel physically tired, but their minds are still racing with thoughts from the day, thoughts about the next day, or just general worries about their lives. When we are stressed, our brains pump out oodles of adrenaline and cortisol; these chemicals in the brain cause the amped up feelings we experience, and even minor amounts take up to twenty minutes to be reabsorbed into the body after calming down. Imagine what it's like if you just stay stressed! Your body is constantly on high alert.

One of the best ways to quiet the mind and encourage sleep is through a relaxation technique known as diaphragmatic breathing (a.k.a. abdominal or deep breathing). This type of breathing is different in that you use your diaphragm to control your breathing, causing the stomach to expand and contract, rather than solely the lungs. This type of breathing can quiet the mind and improve the quality and quantity of sleep.

## Practice Exercise – Deep Breathing

Deep breathing is not complicated, though often feels awkward when you're first learning it. Breathe in through the nose to about a four count and then out through the mouth for a four count.

While learning the breathing technique, you'll want to lie on your back, with one hand on your chest and one hand on your stomach. This will allow you to see your stomach rising and falling, so you know you are implementing the technique correctly. Practice this breathing until it feels natural and you are fully aware of the different sensations. At that point, you no longer need to be on your back or place your hands on your stomach and chest.

Generally, what has worked best for my patients is 10 breaths as described above six times per day on the following schedule:

1. When waking.
2. Mid morning.
3. Lunchtime.
4. Mid afternoon.
5. Dinner time.
6. Before bed.

To assist with sleep, you'll especially want to do the breathing before bed and if you happen to wake up during the night. Over time, you will notice that it has become easier to fall and stay asleep, and that you are waking more rested in the morning.

## Helpful Hints

- If you notice dizziness or hyperventilation, stop and resume normal breathing. Make sure you're not breathing too quickly, too slowly, too deeply, or too shallowly; you'll know you've got it if you start to feel relaxed by your tenth breath.
- The biggest issue for folks typically is simply remembering to do the breathing. Leave yourself notes, set the alarm on your smart phone, or incorporate the breathing with other activities, like taking pills or eating meals/snacks, to help.

*What if you \*still\* can't sleep*

Sometimes making the above changes are not sufficient and you still find yourself experiencing difficulty falling and/or staying asleep. In that case, you can try sleep restriction. This is exactly what it sounds like – restricting the amount of time you spend in bed. The idea is that you only stay in bed the amount of time you are able to remain asleep.

## (Optional) Practice Exercise – Sleep Restriction

Engaging in sleep restriction begins by using a sleep diary to estimate how long you actually sleep for. For example, let's say you lay in bed for eight hours, but only sleep for five; these are the steps for sleep restriction (modify with your own sleep numbers, as appropriate):

1. You are only allowed to be in bed for five hours initially. It doesn't matter if you fall asleep within 30 minutes or four hours. You must get out of bed after five hours.
2. Once you are able to fall asleep within 15-20 minutes of getting into bed and stay asleep for the entire five hours, you would add 15 minutes to your scheduled sleep time every night, until you ran into sleep difficulty again.

3. Then you would stay at that length of time in bed until you were able to fall asleep and stay asleep the entire time, at which point you would resume adding 15 minute blocks until reaching your desired amount of sleep (such as eight hours).

No matter how tired you get, do not take naps when implementing sleep restriction. This will negate all your hard work and further interfere with your sleep patterns.

*Does that sound hard?*

Well, it is definitely challenging. Maintaining sleep restriction when your sleep deprivation actually increases slightly in the beginning results in some people quickly giving up and calling the technique a failure. In fact, the biggest roadblock I've seen with people trying it is giving up in the beginning because of the increase in sleep deprivation. But, typically within a couple of weeks of consistent use, the results speak for themselves.

By the way, in the interests of being able to fully function while trying this technique, it is recommended that you start with a minimum of five hours if possible. If you're truly sleeping less than five hours a night, and would like to start at that point, you may want to only try this technique under the watchful eye of a healthcare provider. Sleep restriction is a challenging but effective way of improving your sleep efficiency. The results are worth it, I promise.

*If you've tried sleep restriction without success...*

You may need to seek outside help. A note about sleep medications. My personal opinion is that, except in the very short-term, they are not a good choice. What I have seen with my own clients are side effects (e.g., increased vivid disturbing dreams); eventual decreased effectiveness of the medication; and not addressing the underlying reason for the sleep disturbance. If you made the above changes and are still having sleep difficulty, there is likely something else going on, whether a sleep disorder, medical issue, or emotional concern that needs to be addressed. Please seek the guidance of a qualified healthcare professional.

## Meditation

As mentioned at the beginning of this chapter, meditation is presented along with sleep because both can be critical to rejuvenation and full functioning. Meditation, by definition, can be any technique that helps the practitioner attain peace, calm, clarity, focused concentration, mental silence, and consciousness changes. Although many techniques can be used, meditation is a non-interactive activity, even if participating with a group. It can involve total silence or may involve repetitive gestures or sounds to assist in focusing. Examples of different types of meditation include:

- Concentration or Focused Meditation designed specifically to assist with sustaining mental focus.
- Mindfulness Meditation designed specifically to improve our ability to live in the moment fully aware of our surroundings.
- Reflective Meditation designed specifically to gain insight on a particular topic through analysis.
- Creative Meditation designed specifically to assist with building character strengths.
- Heart-centered Meditation designed specifically to assist with development of empathy, compassion, and kindness.
- Spiritual or Religious Meditation designed specifically to assist with deepening your connection to your higher power.
- Mantra Motivation designed through use of a repetitive chant to assist with focused concentration.
- More specific types within the above include transcendental meditation, Zen meditation, Buddhist meditation, and Taoist meditation.

*Note that these are simply examples and not nearly an exhaustive list; for example, others distinguish between concentrative and non-concentrative meditation.

Explaining and differentiating between all of the above types of meditation is way beyond the scope of this book. I simply wanted you to be aware that there isn't just one type of meditation. There are tons of options; but here's the key. At the end of the day, my reason for including meditation in this chapter is because meditation is rejuvenating. It has many of the physical and emotional benefits of adequate sleep, with the added bonus of in-the-moment calming whenever you want.

## Practice Exercise – Meditation

The meditation possibilities are practically endless – and you may have recognized that the deep breathing earlier in this chapter can certainly be meditative in practice. Nevertheless, I thought it would be helpful to include a short guided meditation here for you to try. You can either review the example below and do from memory or you can record yourself reading the below (slowly for full benefit) and practice with the recording. Maybe try both and see what works best! Before trying the example, ask yourself how you're feeling right now. Then do the meditation.

## Dr. Silvio's Two Minute Meditation

- Sit comfortably or lie down, whichever feels best for you right now.
- Begin to notice your breathing and concentrate on breathing in through your nose and out through your mouth.
- Breathe in, breathe out, breathe in, breathe out; start to feel your body relaxing with each breath.

- You are standing at the top of a small hill overlooking an empty beach.
- As you take each step down the hill toward the water, feel your body fill with peace and tranquility.
- Feel the sand between your toes as you continue walking, your state of relaxation spreading.
- Feel the sun gently on your skin as you continue walking, feeling completely safe and completely relaxed.
- You reach the water, feeling it softly flow over your feet, the coolness comforting you.
- The sight of the gentle waves bringing the water in and away from you gives you an emotional lift.
- Feeling refreshed, you turn from the water and begin walking the path back up the hill.
- Again you feel the sand between your toes and the sun on your skin, but now you feel more alert and aware.
- With each step you continue your journey back to full awareness, your mind feeling energized.
- As you reach the top of the hill, you feel happy and truly alive, ready to resume your day.
- When you feel ready to leave this scene, open your eyes slowly, taking a few deep breaths, centering yourself.

How do you feel after doing the meditation? Calmer, more alert, something else? Note any positive changes physically, mentally, and/or emotionally, especially positive emotions.

## Helpful Hints

- Repeat this exact meditation daily, or feel free to adapt the daily meditation script in any way that makes it work better for you. I recommend immediately upon awakening, to start your day.
- You also can increase the length of your meditations over time.

There are tons of websites and smart phone apps that can guide you through any length of any type of specific meditation.
- Depending on your identified needs over time, you can look for one of the more specific meditations I listed in the beginning, or stick with the more general ones. There is no right or wrong choice; a meditation is a good one for you if you attain the result you're seeking.

## Vignette

Mike had experienced sleep difficulty for years by the time he came to see me for help. He was uncertain when the trouble had even begun, just that without taking prescribed sleep medication, his sleep was significantly disturbed. He explained that it would take him up to two hours to fall asleep and that he would wake up at least once and sometimes 2-3 times during the night. When he would wake up, sometimes he was able to fall back asleep immediately, but more commonly, he found himself simply staring at the ceiling for up to another hour, wondering when he would fall back asleep.

Since Mike had a reasonably good idea of how much sleep he was getting, the first step in working with him was to analyze his sleep patterns. Without realizing it, Mike had taught his mind and body to associate the bed with being awake by simply laying in bed hoping to fall asleep. Thus, the first thing I did was review the sleep guidelines and recommendations with him. With questioning, I determined that alcohol, nicotine, and caffeine were not related to his difficulty. In addition, his workout schedule and eating habits did not appear to be factors. The main issue was going to bed when he was not tired and remaining in bed, unable to fall asleep.

To assist Mike with retraining his brain to associate the bed with sleep instead of with being awake, we focused on diaphragmatic breathing and getting out of bed when not asleep within 15-20 minutes. I taught Mike the deep breathing technique in session and he practiced until he felt comfortable. I combined the technique with the instruction not to remain in bed if not asleep within 15-20 minutes. Mike was told to engage in the breathing for at least ten breaths, but up to a few minutes to attain a state of relaxation before bed. If he was then not asleep within 15-20 minutes, he was to leave the bed and do something really boring (like reading the phone book) until he felt sleepy. He would do the breathing again and repeat this cycle as needed until he was able to fall asleep within 15-20 minutes. If he awoke during the night, he was to immediately do the breathing. If he didn't fall back asleep within 15-20 minutes, he would use the same cycle as he did at the start of the night until he was able to fall back asleep quickly. The final instruction was to implement this plan for two weeks to allow it time to work, and then come see me again.

Two weeks later, Mike returned with the biggest smile on his face. He reported that the first week was pretty rough. He described getting in and out of bed constantly, doing the breathing technique each time, but still remaining unable to fall asleep within the allotted timeframe. However, he stuck with it, and by the end of the first week, he began to notice that he was falling asleep within 30-60 minutes, instead of 90-120, and he was only waking once during the night and falling back asleep within 30 minutes. By the end of the second week, he was able to fall asleep within about 10 minutes and slept through until his alarm woke him a full eight hours later. Mike reported feeling the most rested he had in years.

## Chapter Purpose

The purpose of this chapter is to start you down the path to sustained ability to stay rejuvenated and restored in your everyday life. Many times I've had patients tell me they are sleep deprived; this is consistent with media reporting. Too many people struggle with poor sleep and too much stress. This chapter hopefully has helped you clean up your sleep habits, improve the amount and quality of your sleep, and incorporate meditation as a stress-reducing, happiness-inducing new habit.

## Practice Exercise Checklist

- Sleep Diary – Before you can possibly make any adjustments to your sleep, you have to determine how much you're really getting. People are notoriously bad at guesstimating this, which is why I recommend keeping a sleep diary for two weeks, where you note when you believe you fell asleep, when you woke up, if you had additional night wakings, or if you took naps during the day. Finally, note how you felt after each night's rest, so you can begin to see how you're truly doing.

- Deep Breathing – As a relaxation exercise, deep breathing can also work wonders for sleep. This version of relaxation breathing asks you to do a minimum of 10 breaths, breathing in through the nose and out through the mouth, six times per day, especially right before bed.

- (Optional) Sleep Restriction – This practice exercise definitely is harder to implement because initially your sleep deprivation will almost certainly worsen. The two main keys to this exercise are limiting yourself initially to the amount of time you estimate you're staying asleep (not just laying in bed) and increasing that amount by increments of 15 minutes until you reach 8 hours (or the amount at which you feel fully rested).

- Meditation – For the final practice exercise in this chapter (and the *Body* section), I ask you to engage in meditation, a fitting crossover activity to the next section, *Mind*. Remember that many options exist for meditation; I included a simple 2 minute guided meditation script for your use (and adaptation, if you wish). I encourage you to try it daily for a couple of weeks and see if you notice a difference in how you're feeling physically, mentally, and/or emotionally.

As your sleep improves, you will no doubt notice a considerable improvement in your mood as well. This is to be expected. Between the healthy eating, regular physical activity, and plentiful sleep, we've covered most of the physical aspect of happiness. It's time to move on to the *Mind*.

# Part 2
# MIND

## STEP 4
## EMOTION REGULATION

*If you would stop, really stop, damning yourself, others, and unkind conditions, you would find it almost impossible to upset yourself emotionally - about anything. Yes, anything.*
Albert Ellis (Psychologist)

As a licensed psychologist, I cannot write about emotion regulation without beginning with cognitive behavioral therapy (CBT). As you read this, it will hopefully make strong intuitive sense (and you may even think, "well, duh") but I want to be fairly explicit so you can understand where I'm coming from and what this whole CBT approach really means. Bottom line: emotions, thoughts, and behaviors are all interconnected. Nothing exists in a vacuum. A flash of thought can trigger an emotion, which results in a specific behavior, which then results in a follow-up thought, or vice versa, in every conceivable order. By the way, if you want considerably more technical information than I intend to provide, read about Aaron T. Beck, Albert Ellis, and BF Skinner; they are a great place to start when researching cognitive and/or behavioral therapies.

*What does this mean?*

It means that with a little bit of work, you can modify your thoughts to change your emotions. Sometimes people get stuck in a negative rut and believe they can't get out (or that they have to take medication to get out). In the vast majority of instances, this simply isn't true. Let me clarify that I am not against medication and, for people who truly need it, medication is indeed a marvel. But, in my opinion, the number of antidepressant and anti-anxiety medication prescriptions suggests they are not being used only when necessary. Plus, many people don't fully realize that medication itself can have a negative impact on mood as a side effect. Medical marijuana is a more recent option and I've seen it have mixed results. Just like pharmaceutical medications, I've seen people become addicted or use it as a crutch instead of learning skills to manage and/or reduce their symptoms. Okay, I'll get off my mini-soapbox now! Back to how you can modify your emotions by modifying your thoughts.

Cognitive-behavioral therapy is based on the idea that the ways we **think** about a person, situation, or event results in our feelings and behaviors, not the external things themselves. This means we can change the way we think to feel and act "better" regardless of the situation. The easiest way to think about this is to realize that if you put, for example, three different people in the exact same situation, you are most likely going to get three different thought processes and emotional reactions. Why is this? People are very quick to state that a particular situation or person "made" them feel a certain way, but in the vast majority of cases, this simply isn't true. Our emotions are a result of our interpretations and thoughts about a given situation, as viewed through the lens of our past experiences.

Let me clarify what I mean. Imagine you are driving down the road and someone enters your lane abruptly, cutting you off. If you were in a car accident a week prior, you're likely to have a thought similar to, "Omigod, that guy almost hit me!" A thought like that is likely to be followed by feelings of anxiety and possibly the behavioral response of slamming on the brakes, or pulling into another lane. If instead, you've had a really terrible day at work and you're just spoiling for a fight, you might be more likely to have the thought, "Hey jerkwad, why don't you watch how you're driving!" This thought is much more likely to be followed by a feeling of indignation and maybe you start tailgating the offender. And, finally, if you're not particularly in a hurry, when the other car cuts you off, you might simply think, "Be careful driving like that", without a strong emotion or a behavioral reaction.

Do you see where I'm going with this? The situation of being cut off was not the **cause** of any of the particular reactions, but rather, the past experiences and immediate thoughts came together to result in specific emotional and behavioral responses. The beautiful consequence of this idea is that it means we ultimately have control over our thoughts, emotions, and behaviors, even when we don't believe we do. We can unlearn unhelpful thoughts and learn ones that result in feelings and outcomes we would prefer. All of this is about your expected outcome and how you would like to feel.

## Cognitive Behavioral Therapy

Cognitive behavioral therapy (CBT) is not a single therapy, but rather an umbrella term that encompasses many other similar types of therapies (for example, behavior therapy, cognitive therapy, and rational emotive therapy). These approaches, while obviously somewhat different, all have as a basic tenet the idea of solving problems related to dysfunctional emotions, unhelpful behaviors, and/or unproductive thoughts by taking a highly goal-oriented approach to alleviating symptoms in the present rather than focusing on the past. CBT emphasizes the role of what we think in terms of how we feel and what we do. This is not Sigmund Freud's endless talk therapy! There is no, "Tell me about your mother" here.

As one might imagine, the exact techniques utilized even within these therapies will vary significantly based on the specific diagnoses or behaviors being targeted. While not therapy, I can provide guidance in adapting therapeutic approaches so that you can assist yourself in managing challenging situations. For example, learning to manage a stressful work environment or resolving relationship conflicts through improved communication; coping with a medical illness itself or the associated chronic physical symptoms; and learning to effectively manage emotions.

## Sometimes All You Need is Movement

Before discussing more involved techniques, let's start at the beginning, with something called behavioral activation. Sometimes just getting yourself up and moving is sufficient to improve mood. This involves topics covered earlier, namely, physical activity and relaxation, but also pleasurable activity. In essence, as discussed before, just being physically active daily can improve your mood. Make sure that you're doing something physically active for at least 30 minutes every day. Relaxation is critical to maintaining a good mood. Hard to be happy when you're tense, right? I won't repeat what was stated in the earlier chapters; just remember that getting a good night's sleep and using techniques like deep breathing and meditation can quite successfully keep you in a relaxed state.

Pleasurable activity requires a tiny bit of expansion. At its core, though, the same recommendation for physical activity applies to pleasurable activity – engage in something fun, either by yourself or with another, for at least thirty minutes every day (remember the adage, all work and no play makes Jack a dull boy? There is considerable truth in that saying!) When people begin to feel stressed, especially when they don't feel there are enough hours in the day, the first thing they tend to do is cut out any activities that don't seem productive or worthwhile. And that almost always involves removing fun stuff. Surprised by that? Or have you been guilty of that exact same reaction?

## Practice Exercise – Pleasurable Activities

What fun activities have you engaged in during the past week, no matter how small? How long did you engage in them? This exercise asks you to develop a retroactive Pleasurable Activities Log. For example, you may have read a book for 30 minutes on Monday and watched a 90 minute movie with your spouse on Wednesday. Whatever fun activities you did, record them below:

| Day & Date | Activity | Length of Time |
|---|---|---|
| | | |
| | | |
| | | |
| | | |
| | | |
| | | |

How was this for you? Did you have something pleasurable to write down for every day of the past week? If yes, that's great. If not, that's okay, keep reading!

A major problem with removing pleasurable activities from your life is that life then becomes drudgery. Once life becomes solely about being productive, the negative thoughts increase, and more pulling back from fun activities ensues. Can you see the downward spiral beginning to take shape here? Unchecked, an individual like this can end up developing symptoms of a mental health disorder, and even if it doesn't go that far, how much fun does this life sound? Not very! Fun is an essential component to daily activity, and in combination with relaxation and regular physical activity, can be just the thing to snap you out of a slump.

## Practice Exercise – Fun Activity Commitment

Now that you have an idea how you're doing with the pleasurable activities, it's time to increase the amount! Think about the fun activities you just wrote down, past activities you enjoyed, or activities you've always wanted to do. Make a commitment to do something fun every single day of the next week. If you are already doing that, based on the above practice exercise, then do two fun activities every day of the next week. What are some options? For example, in the past week, I've read a book, worked in the garden, watched a movie with my husband, played with our cats, went jogging with a group, etc. Consider activities to do alone as well as with other people. Use the same format as in the above practice exercise.

| Day & Date | Activity | Length of Time |
|---|---|---|
| | | |
| | | |
| | | |
| | | |
| | | |
| | | |

How was this for you? Did you have something pleasurable to write down for every day of the week? If yes, that's great. If not, think about what may have interfered...did you struggle to come up with ideas, was it a challenge prioritizing fun? After problem solving what happened, my recommendation is to try the practice exercise again before continuing on in the chapter.

*What if that's not enough?*

Naturally, behavioral activation and relaxation are not always enough to reduce negative emotions and increase positive emotions. That's when more specific cognitive techniques can be beneficial. This involves activities like using positive self-talk (although you may laugh, regularly telling yourself how fabulous you are really can change the way you feel about yourself). The key technique here is paying attention to your physical, emotional, and behavioral responses in different situations. You want to identify your interpretation of the meaning of a given situation, as influenced by your beliefs about the situations themselves, yourself, and other people.

In the beginning, this type of monitoring and change is tough. The goal is to recognize your patterns of thinking and behavior that may be contributing to the negative emotions you're experiencing. Regardless of how long you've felt or acted a certain way, and no matter how normal and "right" it feels to you, if you are not experiencing life the way you would like to, then clearly there is room for change!

## Practice Exercise – Thought Log

Begin keeping a journal or record (you probably noticed I'm a fan of these!) of situations, emotions, and thoughts to determine patterns of unhelpful thoughts and their connections to negative emotions and maladaptive behaviors. Buy a small notepad that you can easily access at any time, or use a method you've used for earlier practice exercises, like the Notes section on your smart phone. Whenever you notice yourself experiencing an increase in a negative emotion, whether sadness, frustration, or worry, get out your notepad or journal and take note of several things (see sample on the next page):

- What is your current situation? Are you at work, in the car, or at home? Include enough detail so that when you read your journal later, you will be able to instantly recall the circumstances of the entry. Don't overdo the details.

- How are you feeling? Try to be as explicit as possible when noting this information. Are you worried, apprehensive, or flat out afraid? Specificity will assist you later in identifying patterns. What is the intensity? On a scale of 1 to 10, where 1 is barely feeling the emotion, and 10 is the worst it's ever been, where are you now?
- What are you thinking? Sometimes these thoughts go by so quickly, we don't believe we've had any, but usually we have. Ask yourself what thoughts immediately preceded the increase in emotion. Try to be as verbatim as possible. This is why you'll want to make your journal entry as close to when you felt the increased emotion as possible – to improve the accuracy of your recollection.

## Helpful Hint

Keep the thought log for at least two weeks, long enough to notice any patterns related to when you are more likely to experience negative emotions; what emotions at what intensity you predominantly experience; and most importantly, what your thoughts are related to these experiences.

## Thought Log

| Date/Time | Situation | Emotion(s) Intensity 1-10 | Immediate thoughts |
|---|---|---|---|
|  |  |  |  |
|  |  |  |  |
|  |  |  |  |
|  |  |  |  |
|  |  |  |  |
|  |  |  |  |
|  |  |  |  |

## Practice Exercise – Thought Challenging

After identifying these thought patterns in the above practice exercise, the next step is to question, or challenge, the thoughts that you've been having. The easiest start is to ask yourself two questions about each of your thoughts identified above:

- Are the thoughts accurate?
- Are the thoughts helpful?

Note the answers to each of those questions on your thoughts from the previous practice exercise. Odds are good that if you experienced a surge in negative emotions after having the thoughts, the answers to one or both of these questions will be "no". The final step then is to consider:

- What is the evidence supporting each thought?
- What is the evidence against each thought?

Consider adjusting your perspective so that you can find a more balanced thought about the situation(s). With balanced thoughts typically come fewer negative emotions.

## Example

This is definitely one of those "easier said than done" situations. Knowledge may be half the battle, but that still means a lot of work to be done! Since employment is so frequently related to negative emotions, let's use a work example for how to analyze your thoughts in a given situation and develop more balanced thoughts.

Your boss comes into your office, hands you back a report you wrote, and tells you that it needs to be completely rewritten. This rarely happens. You notice your temperature climbing, literally and figuratively. Let's analyze this experience:

- Situation – Being told by your boss that your work needs to be redone.
- Emotion – Noting your physical and emotional sensations, we label the current emotion as irritation.
- Intensity – Since the boss rarely returns your work, you feel the irritation strongly, say a 6 out of 10.
- Thought – What is the associated thought? In this example, your thought is, "The boss always hates my work."
- Challenge – Now, ask yourself if this thought is accurate and helpful. Since you don't normally get negative comments from your boss about the poor quality of your work, the thought appears inaccurate. Is the thought helpful? Since your reaction is to become irritated, the answer is probably no.
- Balanced Thought – Having identified our unhelpful and inaccurate thought, the final step is to shift perspective and develop a more balanced thought. What is another way to interpret and think about the situation? When the boss returns your report, telling you it needs to be rewritten, another way to look at it is to assume goodwill; the boss just wants the report to be its best and maybe there truly is room for improvement. Accept the criticism of your work and realize it's not personal. A balanced thought then could be, "The boss has a very specific idea for the writing of this report; now that I know what it is, I can make it spectacular."

*How can this help?*

Negative thinking begets negative thinking. In the example above, can you see how, if you had had the balanced thought initially, you likely would not have experienced the surge of irritation? That's what reframing situations and modifying thoughts ultimately results in – improved mood and reduced negative emotions.

> The more you interpret ambiguous events in a negative light, the easier it becomes to continue to do so.

On the other hand, if you can replace that default negative thinking with more helpful thoughts, over time your new habitual way of thinking will be positive, or at least more balanced. You are basically unlearning bad habits and replacing them with more helpful ones that result in preferred feelings and behavioral outcomes. Keep the thought log as described earlier for as long as it takes for the new ways of thinking to solidify and become habitual.

## Helpful Hints

- Fake it till you make it. While you work on modifying your thoughts and unlearning bad cognitive habits, pretend you've already been successful! Believe it or not, this will make the transition easier.
- Reducing negative emotions can be made even more successful by then working to actually increase positive thoughts. And how can you do that? Read on to find out!

## The Art and Science of Positivity

To me, one of the drawbacks of standard therapy in psychology is the emphasis on sickness. While reducing the negative aspects of a person's thoughts, emotions, and behaviors are important, for many people it is incomplete. Luckily, I am not the only psychologist to have felt that way. Martin Seligman actually developed a branch of psychology called positive psychology. This branch of psychology developed primarily from humanistic psychology.

Just as I wrote with regard to CBT, a full accounting of humanist psychology is outside the scope of this book (see the writings of Abraham Maslow and Carl Rogers for more). However, I do want to introduce humanistic psychology before discussing how the tenets of positive psychology can be helpful to you.

Because I view the world for its possibilities and endeavor to focus on the good within people and society, it was only natural that when studying psychology I was attracted to humanistic psychology. This complementary approach to traditional therapy emphasizes the healthy aspects of the individual. In other words, what is going right for them, as opposed to what is going wrong. The fundamental belief is that people are innately good, and that negative outcomes are the deviations from this natural state. While individuals are recognized as holding the power over their emotional health, humanistic psychology also recognizes the impact of the environment and its influence on our experiences and perceptions. This approach focuses on individuals and their potential as they explore how meanings, values, and personal responsibility play a role in functioning. The ultimate goal is self-actualization, or the full realization of an individual's potential. These are pretty cool ideas. It's no wonder that Martin Seligman took these ideas and ran with them.

## Positive Psychology

It's not just about being happy! Just like humanistic psychology, positive psychology focuses on promoting mental health rather than treating mental illness. The emphasis is on an individual's strengths and how to construct the best life for that individual. Thus, while happiness is a likely outcome, this is only one part of positive psychology. Positive psychology focuses on positive emotions, positive individual traits, and positive institutions as applied to three "types" of life: the pleasant life, the good life, and the meaningful life. A full accounting of positive psychology is outside the scope of this book; Martin Seligman has many books on Amazon.com and/or you can visit the Positive Psychology Center through the University of Pennsylvania website (http://www. http://ppc.sas.upenn.edu/).

## Practice Exercise – Positive Emotions

Positive emotions are pretty much what they sound like, but explicitly applied to one's entire life. Ask yourself the following:

- You can't change the past, but are you pleased, satisfied, or at least content with what has happened?
- Are you happy right now in your present life?
- Do you have hope for the future?

The more you can answer yes to these questions, the more you can say you are living a pleasant life, or a life of enjoyment.

- Do you experience positive feelings through your relationships and interests?

Positive emotions encourage newness in both thoughts and actions and are innately tied into individual traits.

## Practice Exercise – Positive Individual Traits

Positive individual traits focus on what researchers in positive psychology describe as strengths and virtues. This practice exercise will be multi-part, to assist you in identifying your strengths. Classic positive psychology identifies 24 strengths and virtues – and there's even a test to help you identify your primary strengths!

1. Take the VIA Survey of Character Strengths at: https://www.authentichappiness.sas.upenn.edu/testcenter
   For example, when I took the test, I confirmed that my strengths and virtues were, first and foremost, creativity, followed by curiosity, love of learning, vitality, and open-mindedness.

2. Have you ever been so engaged in an activity that you develop almost a sense of tunnel vision? It's only you and the activity, you've lost track of time, you're focused to the exclusion of all external information. Take note of those activities, as they likely involve your strengths identified by the Survey above.

When positive individual traits are applied across work and play, you can create the good life, or life of engagement. True engagement exists when there is a match between a person's particular strength and the task in which they are involved. This is what many people, especially athletes, might refer to as being in the "zone". Mihaly Csikszentmihalyi (one of the leading psychologists interested in positive psychology and happiness) called it "flow" and it includes the idea that activities are the end in themselves, not a means to something else.

## Helpful Hint

A goal of positive psychology is to use your strengths every day in activities that bring you joy; the more you're able to do that, the happier you will likely be. Consider your answers above and brainstorm ways to actively use your strengths and be "in the zone".

Positive institutions focus on those broader concepts that apply to entire communities. This can include concepts such as justice, responsibility, and tolerance. It's through being part of something larger than ourselves, and giving back to that something else, that helps to develop a meaningful life. This type of life is also called a life of affiliation and can include involvement with almost anything, from your family, to a local church, to the entire community. I consider this so important, I devote all of *Step 7* to the idea of community.

By being actively involved in institutions outside of the self, an individual is able to develop a sense of belonging and purpose. Sadly, this is where people seem to struggle. However, it is absolutely critical to developing a positive sense of well-being. The meaningful life helps people see their connection to the broader society and their opportunity to make the world a better place.

How exactly is application of positive psychology going to help you achieve that nebulous term: happiness? Let me directly apply what this means for you. To summarize above, the idea is that experiencing positive emotions lead to the pleasant life, where using your strengths in tasks for which you are a good fit leads to the engaged life, and when this is all done for something outside yourself, can lead to the meaningful life. Positive psychology can help you identify your personal strengths and these will help you shape a life that is truly one worth living. Once you've identified your personal strengths in the practice exercise from earlier, take a good hard look and consider your life's activities:

## Practice Exercise – Applying Positive Psychology

- Is your job merely a paycheck, or do you have a sense of fulfillment at the end of the day? _____

If you only work to play, then you may be mismatched in your job. Ask yourself if you have a job that applies your personal strengths. Brainstorm employment that may be better suited, or consider if there are ways to incorporate your personal strengths in your existing position.

- Do you experience that sense of flow, or being "in the zone", when you play? Do you truly love the activities you claim you do for fun? _____

If not, take a deeper look at why you do the things you do. If you are not experiencing joy every day, it's unlikely that you are using your personal strengths when engaging in pleasurable activities.

- Do you feel a sense of purpose? Do you feel connected to the world around you? _____

If not, look outside yourself; have you joined any groups, do you volunteer, do you give back to the community? Read *Step 7* closely with an eye towards where you can make changes!

Have you heard the pithy saying, "don't just survive, thrive"? By applying the tenets of positive psychology, you can thrive, both as an individual and as a member of a community. By identifying and applying your personal strengths across all aspects of your life, you can increase your sense of well-being and live a happier, more fulfilling life. That's why you're reading this book, isn't it? You aren't looking for just momentary gratification, but long-term satisfaction and happiness. You have it within you to make any changes necessary to achieve authentic happiness. Believe in yourself.

## Building Belief in Yourself

If the above seems impossible, you may have low self confidence. What is self-confidence? Good question!

> Self-confidence is the belief in your own abilities, the certainty that you possess the knowledge, judgment, and power to accomplish your goals.

Sounds lofty, but remember that we all started out with complete self-confidence. Don't believe me? Imagine an infant. Why does she cry? She cries because she's hungry, her diaper is dirty, she wants her caregiver to provide attention. But, most importantly, she cries because she is confident that her cries will be answered, that she will receive what she wants in that moment. Now, we don't typically call it self-confidence because that is a higher-order thought; however, as that infant's needs are met and continue to be met as she grows up, her sense of self-confidence will continue to develop into what we as adults typically see.

If, on the other hand, as she grows up, her needs do not continue to be met, her self-confidence will not flourish, and may even be diminished. And that's how you end up with an adult who does not believe in herself. Her experiences (hurtful words of others, painful life events) have erroneously taught her that she does not have the ability to be successful. Are you that little kid grown up? Do you have self-confidence or self-doubt? Don't worry if you identify with the child with self-doubt, I'm going to provide you with information and steps on how to improve your belief in yourself.

An absolutely crucial first step toward developing self-confidence is to actually *do* something, anything. At times our anxiety can be paralyzing and we find ourselves unable to take even the tiniest of steps forward. Before moving on to the recommendations of how to overcome that anxiety and develop self-confidence, let's start with a very simple idea. If you don't try, you can't be successful. You lose out on every chance you don't take. Nothing ventured, nothing gained. Are you getting the idea? If you don't at least get off the couch to try, you absolutely will not be successful. If you try, and fail, that's okay. You just keep trying. If necessary, involve other people in your endeavors. Many times, people would like assistance, but because they expect to be told no, they never bother to ask. Consider…

## What's the worst that can happen?

The person will say no. So what? If you never ask, you get the same outcome, so what's the drawback to asking? There isn't one. As you ask for help and people provide it (most of the time, people will agree to help if you ask nicely), eventually your expectation begins to turn and you will be confident of receiving assistance. The key is that you have to at least try something.

First, some clarity. We all know individuals who seem to have confidence that they will always succeed, no matter what they do. However, for most folks, our sense of ourselves and confidence in our abilities varies dramatically based on the topic or skill being considered. For example, you may have complete confidence in your ability to do your job – when you're behind your desk working at your computer. If you were to stand before the CEO or the Board of Directors, suddenly you feel like an ill-prepared child called to the front of the classroom. Self-confidence varies. Thus, the first and most general step to improving self-confidence is to identify exactly what you want to improve. Almost everyone experiences some degree of poor self-confidence. Identify your prominent areas of concern and follow the steps and suggestions below. All you need is effort, imagination, and persistence.

## Practice Exercise – Overcoming Fear of Failure

Pick an activity you've procrastinated doing out of fear of failure. This could be as small as asking someone out on a date or as big as launching a new company. If it's a larger overall task, pick a smaller piece to start with. For example, if you want to go back to school, your first step might be identifying options, considering degrees, etc.

What is your chosen activity? _____
_____
_____

Now apply the steps:

   1.   What would it be like if you were already successful?
This step is of critical importance. Imagine the habit you want to have, the task you want to accomplish, the success you are looking for. Now, imagine you've already achieved this goal. An interesting

thing I discovered studying the brain in cognitive psychology is that the pathways in the brain for a vividly imagined event and the real event itself are actually indistinguishable. Use your imagination to see yourself successful. When you imagine the situation, what do you see, what can you physically feel, what do you hear, what can you taste, what do you smell? Visualize yourself acting confidently and successfully in this situation.

2. Now act as though you were already successful.

This is along the lines of the "fake it till you make it" idea expressed earlier. If you act as if you already have the habit, accomplishment, or other success, both your internal and external responses – namely your thoughts and behaviors – will automatically fall in line. You will think, sound, and act as though you are confident in your abilities. You expect success. You don't doubt your ability to accomplish. Over time, your thoughts and behaviors will begin naturally occurring like this – you'll wake up one day to discover you aren't actually faking it anymore!

3. If the self-doubt creeps back in to try to sabotage you, ask yourself – what's the worst that can happen?

There is an interesting idea called anticipatory anxiety. All anxiety comes from a place of not knowing what the future holds. We develop anxiety when we expect or predict that the future holds bad outcomes. That's when we begin to experience self-doubt. But, if you consider just how bad things can get, and ask yourself if this will matter in a year, 5 years, or 50 years, you learn that events we foretell are rarely as bad as we initially imagine. Why waste your energy worrying about something that hasn't happened? Control what you can and let the rest go by not trying to predict the future and keeping the situation in perspective.

4. Spend more time with confident people.

Optimistic confident people see the world differently than pessimistic people do. As you probably learned as a child, we tend to mimic or model, even subconsciously, the behaviors and attitudes of people with whom we spend the most time. Make sure the people you spend time with have the qualities you wish to develop in yourself, namely self-confidence. If you have a specific goal related to self-confidence, you may also find it helpful to identify someone who is already confident and successful in the area you wish to be. Even if this person isn't immediately available to you (perhaps because they're famous), read everything you can about them and try to get any exposure to them that you can (if they give public presentations, for example). Word of caution, be a fan, not a stalker. I'm just saying.

5. In addition to learning from already confident, successful people, it can be helpful to relive your own successful moments.

Almost everybody has had moments where they felt strongly self-confident. Almost everybody has had situations where they felt successful. Relive those moments and situations to remind yourself that you **can** be a confident success. Relive those moments and situations to remind yourself what it **felt** like to be a confident success. If you made past mistakes that are holding you back, let them go by first learning what you could do differently for a better outcome. Then re-imagine those situations so that you are the strongly confident person who created the outcome you desired. As they say, today is the first day of the rest of your life. Remember your successes, learn from your failures, and then move confidently into the future you are creating.

6. Quit telling yourself you can't do it!

All of the above steps are great, but if you continually berate yourself and insist that you will be unsuccessful, that is the outcome you are likely to achieve. There are several concrete ways to shut off that internal critic who keeps insisting you aren't smart, dedicated, or talented enough.

a) Imagine that internal voice differently. If there's someone you admire, who has the qualities you wish to develop, imagine your internal voice sounds like that person. Would that person belittle you? Of course not!

b) Look into the mirror every morning and tell yourself how strong and capable you are, instead of criticizing your imagined flaws.

You will notice an increase in your confidence if you practice the above consistently. We are what we think.

7. Be aware, not only of the negativity and energy-draining thoughts of people around you, but of the negativity and anxiety of society as a whole.

Turn on the television and flip through the various news stations – what do you see? "If it bleeds, it leads". The media will pick the most sensationalist angle for everything. What do you think that does for your own psyche, to be constantly bombarded with stories that seem to basically just suggest the world is going to end? I almost never watch the news because the focus is so intensely negative and directly increases the overall anxious mood of the world. (I don't expect you to remain oblivious to what's going on in the world – but try reading about it on different websites, ideally from different countries. You're more apt to actually get at the truth under the presented images.)

8. Give yourself a whole person makeover.

Obviously, reading this book will help you make external and internal changes. Improve your diet. Increase your physical activity. Learn to relax. Change your thinking. As you're making those changes, consider changing your appearance. Seek advice to update your hairstyle, your wardrobe, even your home decor. When we look good, we feel good. I don't think anybody would dispute that!

9. One of the best ways to boost confidence is to be prepared and have a plan, covered in the *Step 6*.

If you have self-doubt about a specific activity, do your research to be prepared to tackle it. Then, break it down into smaller, less overwhelming pieces. Finally, identify specific goals for each day, week, and month; however big the project may be. This will accomplish several things. First is that the activity will feel a whole lot more manageable. Second is that as you accomplish each of those smaller pieces that make up the whole, you will reinforce the idea that you're perfectly capable of being successful. Finally, the more successes you have at specific tasks, the more you will begin to realize that you are capable of handling anything, whether related to your own personal growth, career, or family and friends. And that's called self-confidence!

## Vignette

Ashley came to me wanting to reduce her level of frustration. She felt that she was not particularly happy, but not exactly sad. What she had noticed most was that she was snapping at her husband, her kids, and her coworkers over the littlest things. She remained in denial about just how irritable she had become until one day her youngest, age 7, asked her, "Mommy, why are you mad at me?" Ashley broke down in tears and immediately came to see me.

Ashley's overall goal was pretty clear and did not require a whole lot of questioning to quantify. She wanted to improve her frustration tolerance, or her ability to manage the minor everyday life stress that previously did not bother her. She specifically wanted to improve her verbal interactions with family, coworkers, and friends. I first worked with Ashley on behavioral activation. Once she successfully increased her level of exercise, utilized relaxation techniques, and engaged in daily pleasurable activities, we reassessed her functioning. She was surprised to notice that she already saw considerable improvement in her mood, especially a decrease in irritability. However, she was still noticing more frustration than she liked, and was beginning to suspect there was some sadness there as well.

Ashley was instructed to begin keeping a thought record. Sometimes clients call these journals, and that's fine, though as you read in this section, clearly a thought record is a little more specific than a journal. I asked Ashley to track her emotions for two weeks. I asked her to make an entry in the record every single time she noticed a negative mood; it didn't matter if it was irritation, sadness, or worry, for example. I encouraged her to record even minor instances of poor mood, as it has been my experience that clients sometimes focus so much on the big emotional events that they miss the frequent minor negative feelings. She was instructed that as soon as possible after noticing negative feelings, that she was to note the date and time, the situation, her mood and the intensity, and most importantly, what thoughts she was aware of directly preceding and during the experience of emotion.

Ashley returned to session two weeks later in a state of shock. Although she was experiencing a fair bit of frustration and irritation, the majority of her entries in the thought record reflected feelings of sadness and discontent. The intensities were rarely high, which is why it took reducing some of the irritation to begin to notice them, but she was a lot sadder than she had even suspected. Ashley had further noticed that much of her sadness seemed to follow predictions of failure.

On her own, as Ashley had noticed the directions of her thoughts, she began naturally to challenge those thoughts. Together in session, we advanced what she had already begun. We practiced challenging her negative associated thoughts, questioning their accuracy and helpfulness. What she noticed was that her thoughts were fairly inaccurate and she worked on finding more balanced thoughts. When Ashley returned to session two weeks later, she looked remarkably happier. She concurred that she was changing her thoughts and that this, indeed, had begun to help her reduce her sadness and resulting irritability. She and I worked for several more sessions until Ashley had no more entries on her thought record that weren't from the normal ups and downs of everyday life.

## Chapter Purpose

The purpose of this chapter is to shake you up a little bit to recognize that you control our emotions and thoughts. Nobody *makes* you happy, sad, or angry. You do that by how you interpret situations and talk to yourself about them. The good news is that you can change this if you want to and are willing to put in the work. The chapter also introduced concepts of positive psychology for increasing happiness and steps for believing in your ability to do, well, anything you set your mind to!

## Practice Exercise Checklist

- Pleasurable Activities – As part of a concept called behavioral activation, retroactively identify and log all of your pleasurable activities from the prior week, noting the day/date, pleasurable activity itself, and the length of time of the activity. Hopefully, there is at least one activity every day, but if not, the next practice exercise addresses that.

- Fun Activity Commitment – Armed with the knowledge from the first practice exercise, make a commitment to engage in more pleasurable activities than you did in the prior week, and a minimum of one per day. Note all of these activities, ideally trying for a mix of solo activities and social activities.

- Thought Log – Begin tracking, for at least two weeks, every situation where you experienced a negative emotion, noting the following: situation, emotion, emotional intensity, and thoughts preceding or occurring during the situation. This will help you to identify your unhelpful thoughts and thought patterns.

- Thought Challenging – This practice exercise is probably one of the toughest in book, let alone in this *Step*. Your goal is to challenge the thoughts identified in your Thought Log by asking yourself if the thoughts are accurate and/or helpful and then identifying more balanced thoughts, likely taking another perspective.

- Positive Emotions – Consider your feelings about your past, present, and future, as well as your feelings about your relationships and activities. The goal is to develop positive emotions in all of these areas and this practice exercise will help you in determining where to focus your energy.

- Positive Individual Traits – Time to identify and consider your use of your character strengths. This multi-part practice exercise asks you to go online and take a strengths test and then consider how you do or do not use those strengths in your everyday activities. Ultimately your goal is to use your positive individual strengths every single day.

- Applying Positive Psychology – You want to thrive, not just survive. Consider why you engage in the activities you do, whether work or play. Brainstorm ways to modify, adapt, or replace activities that are not using your highest strengths and giving you a sense of fulfillment and connection to the world.

- Overcoming Fear of Failure – The final practice exercise of the chapter asks you to pick an activity, big or small, you've procrastinated doing out of fear of failure. After identifying the activity (or a small chunk of it to start with), you are then to apply the nine steps to assist you with actually accomplishing that activity and moving forward successfully.

Note: You *can* regulate your emotions and feel the way you want to feel. It may take considerable effort, depending on where you are at the start, but you can be successful. However, if you take all of these steps and find that you still aren't where you want to be, or if you find you are having thoughts of wanting to hurt yourself or someone else, make the healthy choice and go see a professional. It may be very scary to take that chance, but, even if you struggle to believe it, you are worth it and you can get the help and support that you need.

# STEP 5
# WHO ARE YOU?

*The privilege of a lifetime is to become who you truly are.*
Carl G. Jung (Psychologist)

Now that you understand the power of your thoughts, let's broaden our scope to actively consider your very nature. Essentially, you need to figure out who you are and who you want to be. *Step 5* will explore doing just that, speaking first to the idea of being comfortable with who you are. Next, I'll talk about how to live true to your authentic self. Then, I'll write about the idea of using/working your goals and desires to be the best "you" that you can be. And, finally, I'll tie it all together as we discuss creating a life plan that will allow all of this to be real. Are you ready?? Are you excited?? Then let's go!

## Be Authentic

You may be thinking, what exactly does she mean by "be authentic"? Various dictionaries define authentic to mean, "genuine, real, not copied, verified, and reliable". When discussing authenticity here, I'll be essentially expanding on all of those definitions to encourage you to be authentic in the sense of living your life according to your own needs and desires, and not the ones placed upon you by the individuals and culture around you. The authentic you does not continue to be limited by the beliefs or conditioning you've developed and created throughout your life as ways to protect yourself and move through the world without getting hurt. It may be safer and more secure, to a degree, but the authentic you strips that aside to be the real you.

*What if you feel authentic?*

You may feel like you're absolutely authentic, that every choice you make is yours alone and not guided and constructed by everything that came before. You may feel that way, but chances are you are wrong. Think of it like playing a role. Do you act the same at work as you do at home? Around your family as your friends? Do you try to present yourself a specific way, depending on the audience? To a certain degree, this is indeed helpful to improve your functioning in the world (for example, it's probably not good to ask for a beer and popcorn at a board meeting, even though you might do this while watching a game with your friends). It's okay to be aware of your surroundings and have situational awareness on how to behave. But if you do this too much, or you find that you have lost your true essence, then it may be time for all of the roles to be reconsidered.

Think about it. You've possibly met a truly authentic person once or twice in your life. These are people who naturally draw the attention of others because they just seem more real than the people around them. They do what they think is right, regardless of outcome, and they speak their minds without worrying what others think of them. Keep in mind that this is distinct from the people who act as though they do not care what others think of them, but it's actually either an attempt to prevent themselves from being hurt or they're just not considerate of others' feelings. These people are not being authentic. Authentic people expose themselves more than anyone else ever could, because they are being real.

*How do you separate the real from the false?*

Look to yourself and look to the people you encounter every day. If you're honest, you know that almost nobody is authentic, that all of us are faking, at least to some degree. Think about what I wrote a second ago – modifying behavior according to circumstances. If you're at a job interview or at work smiling after your brother died…you will present a certain face to your audience because it is expected and because you are hiding. Now, like I also wrote earlier, this is more comfortable for most people and you may not want to release these masks because it will make many aspects of life more uncomfortable. But, think about how stressful it can be to *always* present what you think the world wants to see, instead of who you truly are.

Many of our approaches to the world go as far back as childhood, as ways we developed to protect ourselves from a world that, frankly, can be scary and painful. As you get older and situations change, many of these approaches are no longer relevant and in fact can hold you back. I've seen the extreme of this in therapy. I have had patients build up incredible walls and only present a smiling, happy persona to the world, in order to protect themselves from being hurt further.

The roles we play become like a surface self – it's how we define ourselves. When someone asks you who you are, how are you most likely to answer? Most folks answer first with their names and then with what they do. If the person continues to ask questions about who you are, you may also answer with who your affiliations are and where you live. None of these are wrong answers, exactly, but they aren't really you, either. These are the surface answers: what you do, where you are in society, things like that. We typically further describe ourselves in terms of those surface wants, needs, and behaviors. "I want to be a doctor." "I want to get married."

What do you think would happen if you answered the question with, "I am an outgoing individual who endeavors everyday to make the world a better place by reducing suffering and increasing happiness". You can imagine the reaction, right? The person asking the question would likely look confused that you didn't follow the script, mumble something about that sounding nice, and then would scurry away as quickly as possible. Clearly, we all play into this drama of life. We get immediate feedback when we aren't playing the game.

## Practice Exercise – Identifying the Mask

How can you know what mask you're wearing? I'm going to ask you to engage in some possibly uncomfortable inner searching. Answer the following as honestly as possible:

- Why do you have the job you hold? _____
  _____

- Why did you study the topic you did in college? _____
  _____

- To that point, why did you even go to college (or not)? _____
  _____

- Why do you behave the way you do around family and friends? _____
  _____

- What do you think of the above answers; why are you doing most of what you're doing? For yourself, for family, for society? _____
  _____
  _____

If you feel incomplete, living the roles family, friends, and society have prescribed for you to play; if you are performing your assigned role instead of tearing away the mask and doing what you love; if you do not feel truly happy and fulfilled, then you are living only on the surface. It's time to dig deep, to the true core of who you are, to discover your unique self and not just continue to play the roles in which you have been cast.

*Do you really know yourself?*

The easiest answer is yes, but the authentic answer is probably no. That's okay, because that's why I'm here, to assist you in being able to answer yes! The first step is to commit yourself to being authentic.

## Do you really want to be authentic?

If yes, then the second step is to take this to heart: stop acting. In everything you do, remember that you don't have to play any roles. You can be yourself. Just stop acting – as if you're happy when you're not, that you're better than someone else when you're not, that you're perfect when you're not.

## Practice Exercise – Discovering Authenticity

Consider the following specific steps and questions to help you stop acting and discover that authentic you buried way down deep:

1. When you are all alone, how do you act? Do you present yourself the same to another as you would to a mirror? Or do you think differently, act differently, speak differently? How come? Why or why not? _____

_____
_____
_____

2. Begin to look deeper and listen to your inner self. You know I'm a believer in journaling; start to chronicle feelings and desires you experience. When do you feel the happiest, the most content, the most challenged (in a good way)? _____
_____
_____
_____

3. Pay attention to your most commonly used self-talk and you may uncover some of your thinking patterns, often originating in childhood, that are critical to maintaining surface roles. What are your thinking patterns related to expectations? _____
_____
_____
_____

4. What are the surface roles you play at work, with friends, with family, with society? For example, at work, you may be the helper. At home, you may be the scapegoat, blamed whenever anything that could go wrong does. _____
_____
_____
_____

5. Remember that not all surface roles are automatically inauthentic. What, if any, of your above surface roles are actually authentic? For example, maybe as a lawyer, you realize that you value fairness and justice; perhaps specializing in animal welfare law would be a better fit to your authentic self? _____
_____
_____
_____

## Helpful Hint

Act as if you are your authentic self. As I'll emphasize next chapter, all the plans in the world are great but ultimately mean nothing if you don't act. That sentiment absolutely applies here as well. All of the insights you've gained as to who you are will mean very little if you don't make changes in the way you think, act, and live your life. That's okay if you're unsure how to implement these newfound discoveries of yourself (or if they still feel insubstantial)...you will know exactly how to proceed by the end of *Step 5*. I promise!

## Who Do You Want to Be?

Remember the age-old question, "What do you want to be when you grow up?" When was the last time somebody asked you that question? Most likely you really were a child and it was some adult who thought you'd give a cutesy answer, like, "I want to be a ballerina". Or you might have been a little older, maybe even high school, and it was a guidance counselor trying to determine the best way to guide you professionally toward that answer. If you had the experience of both, just comparing those two will demonstrate how much the intent of those questions and their answers can change. Now imagine being asked that question as an adult. What would be your answer and what would be the reaction of the person asking the question?

As a child you were free to be who you were and to daydream about what you wanted to be when you grew up, because nobody (hopefully) told you that you couldn't. You never heard, "That's impossible", or "impractical", or "foolish". Odds are, though, that if you answered the same way when asked as a child versus when asked in high school, unless the answer was a ridiculously practical, socially-preferred occupation, like, "I want to be a banker", you probably didn't get a ton of support. And, if you were crazy enough to answer the same way as an adult, you possibly would get eye rolls or even a chuckle or two.

## Why is the response to your answer to the question of "What do you want to be?" different just because you have a driver's license and a mortgage?

Most people want to be happy when they grow up (which is why you're reading this book!) As a child, you don't really think about it, but maybe it just sounds cool to be a cowboy. But, if you were able to think introspectively as a child, undoubtedly you would discover that the reason you liked the cool answers was because you believed that being a cowboy would lead to happiness.

### Practice Exercise – Finding Your Purpose

What do you want to be when you grow up? Answer the following without overanalyzing, if possible:

1. How did you answer the question of "what do you want to be when you grow up" when you were a child? _____
   _____
   _____
   _____

2. Ask yourself, just generally, "What do I love to do?", even as a hobby?_____
   _____
   _____
   _____

3. If you daydream about your daily life, what do you imagine yourself doing? _____
_____
_____
_____

4. What skills and talents do you already possess? _____
_____
_____
_____

5. If you didn't have to worry about being successful (whatever that means to you), or about paying your bills, or about what other people think about your choices, what would you absolutely love to do? _____
_____
_____
_____

6. What do your friends and family think you're good at? _____
_____
_____
_____

The key to the above practice exercise is that, for example, you may no longer really want to be a cowboy, but it may help remind you of the passion you once felt when you looked to the future. On the other hand, you may realize that, yeah, you really do still want to be an actress, an entrepreneur, or a rocket scientist. Same with what you do now for fun. It may not tell you exactly what direction to go in, but there are undoubtedly some clues!

## Helpful Hint

If you were really scratching your head with some of those questions, that's okay. Sometimes people didn't have burning desires as children or really aren't sure what they enjoy as adults. Maybe you truly are just floating through life without any clear ideas. If that's you, then focus on question #6 above; if you're still unsure, directly ask your friends and family. Sometimes other people can see things from that outside perspective that we'd never see ourselves. You may be surprised at the answers that you get!

*Do you think you have the answer to the question?*
That's wonderful! Now it's time to put it into action. You'll learn more when we discuss goals next chapter; for now, realize if you don't have an idea of a goal, it becomes nearly impossible to create a path to success. As you decide on what you have as a dream or goal, remember what I wrote in the *Introduction* to this book: Dreams are the reality you have yet to create. Dream big!

## Practice Exercise – Dreaming Big

Because you are an adult, when you think about your answer to the question of what you want to be when you grow up, there are other considerations. All actions have consequences; it can be helpful to consider those possibilities. Your answers to the following will help you in determining what you may or may not want to do, and exactly how best to accomplish that. If you are now considering making a change, how will that change possibly impact your:

1. Current work and career? _____
   _____

2. Play or pleasurable activities? _____
   _____

3. Relationships/family? _____

_____

4. Finances? _____

_____

I'm not asking you to consider these impacts because I intend to tell you that your life dream isn't practical. Of course not! But, I am telling you to be thoughtful as you move forward. If you're married with four kids and pay your mortgage on your income, quitting your job to be a street artist may be too bold a first step!

By using the skills you'll learn in the next chapter, you can develop a very specific plan, filled with short- and long-term goals that will help you achieve your answer to the question of what you want to be when you grow up. For now: Take a first step. It's really just as simple as that. What might that entail? Let's say that when you think about what you loved as a child, you realized it was animals. You remember at various times stating that you wanted to be a veterinarian, marine biologist, zookeeper. When you think about the theme that tied everything together, it truly was a love of animals. Reflecting on how you feel today, you realize that you want to help animals on a larger scale. In fact, you realize that you want to be a lawyer specializing in animal welfare. Okay, let's go!

After you create your plan with all of your specific goals, it might look something like this...

*Consider volunteering or interning.* For example, you start by volunteering at the local humane society, helping to socialize the animals. Or you become more actively involved in grassroots animal welfare issues, such as writing your Congressman about the evils of dog-fighting.

*Identify any necessary education or experience.* For example, you need a degree in law to become an attorney. So, you identify law schools with specialties in animal law, determining what works geographically.

*Determine the most effective way to move toward your goal given your life situation.* For example, you decide that you can afford to live on savings while you attend school; or maybe not, and you take night classes instead.

And so on and so forth. Do you get the idea? Just make a change! Plan your transition to the life you want. This may entail a gradual transition, or it may be a jumping in with both feet kind of transition, depending on your own personal temperament and current life situation. Either one is fine, as long as you have a plan and are moving forward, toward creating the life you want.

Remember that words are powerful. What you say will become reality. You can use this to your advantage by owning your desires and putting it out to the world. Allow the energy of the universe to work for you and help manifest the life you want. When people ask you who you are, answer proudly. "I am a writer." "I am a veterinarian." "I am a cowboy." Make it real!

## Practice Exercise – Creating Your Life Plan

For the final exercise of the chapter, I want you to put everything together from the beginning of this chapter up to now and work through the following steps, using your answers from earlier as well:

1. Assess. Start with an honest self-assessment of who and where you are. Do you feel incomplete? Do you feel you are performing assigned roles more than being your authentic self?

2. Find your bliss. If you didn't have to worry about being successful (whatever that means to you), about paying your bills, or about what other people think about your choices, what would you absolutely love to do?

3. Make considered plans. Consider your current life circumstances as you decide how best to move forward. Don't worry if it's a little vague right now. You'll gain skills in the next chapter to plan your transition, whether slowly or in giant leaps forward.

4. Take a first step. Start small, engaging in new hobbies, volunteering, or interning, as you learn about new (or old) loves. When you're ready, if you wish to, go ahead and make bigger changes by returning to school or beginning a new part- or full-time job.

## Vignette

Lucy appeared to the world as a very successful businesswoman, happily married mother of three, and active member of her church. As I was reminded when Lucy sought my services, images can be deceiving. Initially, she stated that she just wanted to feel "something" again. Delving a little deeper, however, I discovered that Lucy felt empty. She loved her family very much, but otherwise believed something was missing.

When asked, Lucy was unable to identify when she noticed her feelings going awry. Nor could she pinpoint exactly what the problem was – as she acknowledged quite openly, she was living the dream. Yet, why wasn't she happy? What was missing? Lucy was very open to exploring what was wrong and what she could do to feel good again.

I started by gently pushing Lucy to examine her thoughts and behaviors. I asked her how she acted when she was all alone versus in a board meeting versus at church versus at home with her husband and children. She quickly realized that she was indeed thinking, acting, and speaking differently in all of these instances. She also realized that while some of that she was comfortable with, much of it she was not. She was ready to work on improving her authenticity.

First I asked Lucy to consider when she felt the happiest. She struggled quite a bit with that, so I modified the question. I asked her instead to think about what she enjoyed as a child. What did she want to be when she grew up? She surprised herself here when she immediately responded, park ranger. She had forgotten that long ago love. Together we explored what was so enticing about being a park ranger as a child and whether it had any ongoing resonance for Lucy as an adult. That's when she had her light bulb moment! Lucy felt happiest when she was outside in nature. Being cooped up inside for nearly all of her activities (including even working out at the gym) meant that she spent almost no time outside.

Lucy knew that she would not choose to make large sweeping changes due to her responsibilities as CEO and mother, so she started small. She began exercising outside; she volunteered to coach her son's soccer team; and she decided to learn (and teach her family about) camping. Within a few months, Lucy had implemented all of these changes and reported a complete turnaround in her life. Lucy had thought she might eventually want to ditch her company and do something in nature as a career. However, she realized after making the other changes that it wasn't necessary. Those seemingly small changes were enough to reignite her. She also began making a more concerted effort to bring those desires into the home and work, for example, by embodying the phrase "reduce, reuse, and recycle". She felt like a new woman.

## Chapter Purpose

Everyone has a face they present to the world, and usually different faces for different audiences. To some extent that may be a good thing. However, it may also be inauthentic to the point that you have lost who you are and what you want to be in the world. The purpose of this chapter was to help you figure out who you are and who you want to be. *Step 5* explored the idea of being comfortable with who you are, or being authentic, and living true to who that authentic person is in part by creating a life plan.

## Practice Exercise Checklist

- Identifying the Mask – In order to live a full, authentic life we first need to identify our lack of authenticity. This practice exercise encourages you to directly question why you do what you do, both now and in the past.

- Discovering Authenticity – Taking the answers from the Identifying the Mask practice exercise and delving deeper, now consider how you act around others, when you're happiest, what kind of self-talk you engage in, and analyzing your surface roles.

- Finding Your Purpose – A big piece to living authentically is to determine what activity would bring you the most happiness. Consider your childhood dreams, your current daydreams, and what you (maybe secretly!) have always wanted to do.

- Dreaming Big – Obviously, implementing your dreams will have a huge impact on your life. While ideally this is mostly for the good, if you are now considering making a change, it can be helpful to consider how that change will possibly impact your current work and career; play or pleasurable activities; relationships; and finances.

- Creating Your Life Plan – Finally, put everything together, using relevant answers from earlier practice exercises to assess yourself, find your bliss, make a beginning plan, and take a first step toward living the life of your dreams.

No matter which steps you follow, how big or small the changes you make in your life are, remember to always stay aware of your thoughts, behaviors, and emotions, and how these either support or hinder your happiness. See yourself as whatever you want to be. Remember that words are powerful. Practice telling yourself and others what you are and what you want to be. Shout it from the rooftops if you want. Be your dream!

# STEP 6
# PLANNING

*A goal without a plan is just a wish.*
Antoine de Saint-Exupery (French writer, including *Le Petit Prince*)

I'm a big fan of quotes and the above quote perfectly captures the importance of this chapter. If you don't have a plan to accomplish your goals, it really is just wishful thinking with minimal chance of success. Planning is the process by which you can accomplish your goals. It provides a map for how to create your success. Planning is based on your specific objectives and the resources you have available to you. Whether you are ultimately successful or not, you will either be able to celebrate the achievement, or be able to identify progress made and lessons learned for next time. And, there will almost always be a next time as you move through life and identify new goals, big and small.

*A plan by any other name?*

Not all plans are created equal. We develop plans for the short- and long-term, related to our specific goals (goal-setting is discussed in the next section). A plan can provide structure as well as motivation. It shows you (and anyone else you care to show it to) that you mean business. It offers clarity and focus initially, plus expectations against which to compare your actual success. Although there are always those dumb luck examples, the bottom line is that while a plan doesn't guarantee success, the lack of a plan can just about guarantee failure. Of course, no two plans are alike, but they all involve the same overall development process – determining your goals, considering possible avenues for success, and deciding on a path to follow.

*What's first?*
A plan must have objectives.
- Why are you creating a plan?
- What are you hoping to accomplish?

Without explicitly identifying and quantifying what you intend to accomplish, you could wind up spinning your wheels. It can be as simple as an unwritten plan to tackle a particularly over-stuffed bedroom closet or as complicated as a researched business plan for developing and starting a new small business. I suspect for the most part, your plans will be for activities somewhere in the middle. Although I could be wrong; maybe someone reading this will be the next Bill Gates! Always keep in mind that identifying realistic and specific goals works best.

*Be realistic!*
Many people directly told me, or indirectly implied, that my goal to become a working writer was unrealistic. "Have a backup plan", I heard repeatedly. When I write that your goal must be realistic, it must be something that is possible to attain. It's irrelevant if it's difficult, but it must be possible. For example, if your goal is to live on Jupiter, that goal is truly unrealistic. But, if your goal is to become a working artist, that's hard but not impossible. Just understand that some goals will require more planning and, frankly, just a little bit of luck.

*How specific do the goals need to be?*

As stated, some plans are fairly simple, and need not even be written down, whereas others are the definition of complicated, involving considerable research and, um, planning. That's some meta-thinking for you – planning your plan. Your goals need to be specific in large part to help you evaluate your process and eventual success.

## How will you know if you've achieved your goal if you aren't even really sure what it is?

When I created my plan to become a working writer, it had many parts. There were items I could directly control (e.g., I would complete the first draft of my new book by a certain deadline). There were items that I could approach but ultimately were in someone else's hands (e.g., I can market my books – now numbering five – but whether or not people buy any of them remains unknowable and unpredictable). For more complicated multipart plans, research what you can, plan for every conceivable challenge, and then work for the outcome you desire.

## Where do you see yourself in five years?

That question sometimes strikes fear in the hearts of people because the possibilities of life can occasionally seem overwhelming or at the least unknowable. But, there's another way to look at that question. It can be quite helpful to recognize that there are different types of goals that work together to assure forward momentum towards your preferred future. Think about your answers to practice exercises in *Step 5* as you move forward. In this next section, I'll present long- and short-term goals, including definition, development, and interrelation.

*What is a long-term goal?*

In our discussions under planning, we spoke of the necessity of having specific, concrete goals. Let's delve into that a little bit more. A long-term goal is any aspiration you have that is a bit off in the distance. How do I make sure those goals are specific and concrete?

I've worked with clients who've said their goals are to be rich or to be healthy, for example. Hmm, well, that's wonderful, but what exactly does that mean? So you want to be rich…does that mean you want a six-figure income, own a vacation island, or have one million dollars in the bank? Just stating you want to be rich is only a starting point and is way too vague to use as a long-term goal. Same with a goal of being healthy. What does that mean? For many people it includes being thinner. But even that is too vague. How much weight do you want to lose? Five pounds? Twenty-five pounds? You won't be able to break your long-term goal into multiple short-term goals (discussed later) if you don't really have a defined end state to identify progress and success.

You'll have a start date (today!), but for many long-term goals you won't necessarily have a completion date. This is because, even if you know exactly what your goal is, there may be so many factors outside of your control, that you can't really predict when you'll reach that preferred end-state. Some goals do have completion dates automatically built in, for example, if you've agreed to a contract or if you've enrolled in a degree program. Although even these may not be set in stone (there just may be consequences if you don't meet the deadlines).

## Practice Exercise – Imagining Your Ideal Life

Ask yourself a question. If you woke up tomorrow and had your ideal life, what would it look like? _____

_____

_____

If you draw a bit of a blank with this one, give yourself some space to be adventurous. Ask yourself, what would I do if I was guaranteed success, or at least there was a very slim chance I would fail? Now go back to the blank space above, and fill that answer in. Use your answer to develop specific long-term goals; what are some of those goals? _____

_____

_____

_____

For example, if your ideal life involved getting up in the morning without an alarm clock, having breakfast with your spouse and children, before heading off to a day of working with animals, this provides all of the information you need to start developing your long-term goals.

Hopefully you recognized that the image you conjured of your ideal life isn't necessarily exactly what you'll choose for your long-term goals (though it could have been). What this exercise absolutely does is help you identify where your bliss can be found. In this example, it becomes obvious that family time and giving back to the community are the key pieces to an ideal life. The next step would be to analyze your current life to see where you are already, where you want to be, and where there's room for changes. Use this to identify long-term goals, such as earning a college degree or having enough money in the bank to retire.

Long-term goals typically seem the most important because they are the path to the lives we hope to be living. The problem of course is that they are so far in the future. As a result we can begin to lose focus on them, or become discouraged as they seem to become unattainable. Short-term goals are those intermediary goals that can be developed to specifically help us achieve our desired long-term goals. Naturally there are short-term goals (such as cleaning out a closet) that are possibly unrelated to our long-term goals, but the key here is to recognize that short-term goals are the stones on the path to our long-term goals. Long-term goals provide the focus, while short-term goals provide the method.

*What is a short-term goal?*

A short-term goal is an objective expected to be met or concluded within a short period of time. What exactly does that mean? Well, it does not refer necessarily to a specific period of time; I've seen it refer to a period of time anywhere from the same day to as long as a year. Most of the work written about goals seems to indicate that anything longer than a year can probably be considered long-term, so for our purposes we'll use that same time frame. Anything that you would like to accomplish within the year is a short-term goal.

Unlike long-term goals, short-term goals, almost by definition, have specific start and stop dates. Why is this? Because these goals are smaller in scope, it's critically important to know when you will start working toward the goal so you avoid procrastination. And you want to know your anticipated completion date so you can review your progress and meet both internal and external deadlines. Make sure you give yourself enough time to not add unneeded stress to the process.

*How do you develop and structure short-term goals?*

The key to developing short-term goals is to first take your identified long-term goal and work backwards from that end-point to where you are today. Once you've done that, you can develop your short-term goals by identifying what you'd like to accomplish today, next week, next month, in six months, and in a year. Of course, you don't have to be that rigid with your time frames; the idea is to remain open to different lengths of time and not get stuck.

I will use the hypothetical long-term goal to be rich, as evidenced by having one million dollars in the bank, to demonstrate development of short-term goals in the service of a long-term goal. If you think about that rather lofty goal, it could be easy to become overwhelmed. But, fear not! Let's break that down.

- What can I do for this goal in the next month? You increase the amount of money you have in savings by either increasing your income or decreasing your expenditures. Let's go with decreasing your expenditures. Beginning this month, you can eliminate buying an expensive specialty coffee every morning on your way to work; and to make sure you actually save that money, set up an automatic monthly transfer from your checking account to your savings account for the amount you won't be spending.
- What can I do in the next six months? Still considering decreasing expenditures, take a look at longer term contracts, like phone, cable, and insurance. You can review each of these contracts and plan to make cancellations or modifications in the next six months to reduce the amount of money going out the door.
- What are some potential roadblocks to achieving each of these short-term goals?
    o For eliminating specialty coffee in the morning: People seem to love their specialty coffees, so one potential roadblock is maintaining the willpower to not be lured in when you drive by the coffee shops every morning. Anticipating this, you can brew coffee at home and have a cup in your car each morning before you leave for work.
    o For reviewing and modifying contracts: Lack of motivation would probably be the biggest roadblock here, as reading over your contracts, contacting each individual company, and negotiating new rates (or being willing to cancel completely) are all time-consuming and possibly conflict-ridden. Overcome that roadblock by breaking this short-term goal into even shorter-term goals: give

yourself one month to review and act on each contract, breaking that goal down even further if necessary (one week to review the contract, one week to contact the company, you get the idea).

## Practice Exercise – Short-Term Goals

Now it's your turn. How do you identify what you'd like to accomplish? Start by using at least one long-term goal you identified related to your imagined ideal life in the earlier practice exercise. With that long-term goal in mind, consider the above section and example, and ask yourself the following questions:

1. What can I do today to move toward this goal? _____
_____

2. What can I do next week to move toward this goal? _____
_____

3. What can I do within the month to move toward this goal? \_\_\_\_
_____

4. What can I do in the next six months? _____
_____

5. What are some potential roadblocks to achieving each of these short-term goals that lead to my long-term goal? _____
_____
_____

As you answer each of these questions, be as concrete and specific as you were in developing the original long-term goal. Similarly, set soft (meaning flexible) deadlines to complete each individual piece.

*Some general guidelines...*

Here are three general guidelines that apply to all goals, short- and long-term. Note that there are articles, chapters, and whole books discussing this topic, but much of it can be summarized in these three steps:

1. Specificity. The absolute number one rule of thumb, for any kind of goal, is to make it specific. As discussed earlier, "I want to be rich" may sound like a long-term goal, but is clearly not specific enough. "I want to have one million dollars in the bank" is much better. For the short-term goals to help you achieve that long-term goal, "I'll save extra money each month" may also sound good, but again is not specific enough. "I will eliminate my specialty coffee on the way to work and transfer that saved $50 per month from my checking account into my savings account" is better.

2. Timely. Once you've established your goals, determine when you'll start working toward them and when you expect to complete them. This accomplishes two things. It helps you evaluate whether your goals can realistically be met within your time frame and helps you avoid procrastination. "I will set up my monthly automatic bank transfer for $50 from checking to savings by the end of the week" is much more likely to lead to successful completion than "I will transfer funds from checking to savings every month."

3. Monitor. Establishing excellent goals and following all of the guidance offered so far will mean little if you don't ever monitor your progress. This includes having a measurable outcome – what's the point in developing a specific goal if you have a vague definition of success! You will need to track your goals and progress made toward each of them so that you don't lose sight of what you're hoping to accomplish. Then you can cross successfully completed goals off the list. I think all of you list makers out there know what I mean when I write about how good it feels to cross items off your to-do list!

## Helpful Hints

- Remember that short-term goals are developed in relation to long-term goals; many short-term goals exist solely in service of your long-term goals.
- Long-term goals thus rely on your success in completing short-term goals. Without short-term goals, long-term goals likely will seem lofty, distant, and unattainable. Short-term goals are the baby steps to get you there.
- Short-term goals without long-term goals can lead to feeling mired and directionless. Truly you cannot have one without the other.

## Practice Exercise – Identifying Parts of Your Goal

Consider goals to be successes that haven't yet occurred. Now that you've considered your ideal life, as well as developed long-term and short-term goals related to it, let's practice the entire sequence on a problem in your life currently. Identify a goal and work through these basic steps for planning:

1. What is the problem you are trying to solve? What is your purpose in creating a plan? _____
_____
_____

All goals are developed to meet a need. What needs do you have? Again, it can be simple or complex. Are you broke? Are you unhappy? Articulate as best you can what the problem is that prompted the desire to make changes.

2. What are the parameters of this problem? It's of critical importance to understand the true nature of your problem. Write

down everything you can think of. _____
_____
_____

For example, if the problem is that you're broke, begin thinking of what exactly that means. Are you unemployed/underemployed? Are your expenses too high? Do you have champagne and caviar tastes when you need a beer and hot dogs budget (to paraphrase Eisenhower)? Forget your usual activities while you take time out to solve your problem. Give this the importance it deserves, but be careful not to get too caught up in the details during this step.

3. Where do you want to be? _____
_____
_____

Considering what problem you are trying to solve, in the context of what it would look like once solved, will help you to develop your goals. A version of what I asked you earlier – what would your life look like if this were no longer a problem? Goals are the potential solutions to your problems. For example, if in the last step, you determined that your expenses are too high, is the issue that you buy things for yourself or others that you can't afford, or perhaps have lots of expensive items like premium cable? Visualize how your life will be once you have accomplished these goals.

4. What are your goals? _____
_____
_____

After you've explored the differences between your current life and the one you would prefer to live, you will be able to identify a specific goal or interrelated goals. For example, once you determine that your income really is adequate, but that you have not been living within your means, you can perhaps identify developing a budget as a goal. This would allow you to manage all of your expenses effectively.

5. How can you accomplish your goal? Write down your specific goal, or each interrelated goal if you identified several. Under each goal, write down what it would take to turn that goal into reality. How do you intend to achieve your goal(s)? If you have multiple interrelated goals, what order is best for accomplishing them?

_____
_____
_____
_____

Once you have your goal(s), break it down into smaller pieces. Give yourself a timeline for accomplishing each individual piece of each specific goal. Be realistic when you do this, based on your background knowledge and skills; for example, if you've never kept a budget, giving yourself only one day to research budgeting programs and master your new budget may set you up for failure.

Remember that the plan is truly just the beginning. Just because you created your beautiful new plan does not mean it will work perfectly without further effort or adjustment. After the initial development, leave it alone to percolate for a bit and change anything that, upon reflection, seems not quite right. In addition, as you make adjustments, try to anticipate where things might go off track and develop contingency plans. For example, as you develop your budget, consider that you have a 10-year-old car that may need costly repairs. Increasing the amount you put into savings to offset unexpected expenses might be the ticket.

When providing individual therapy, every now and again I get a patient who feels odd writing down whatever I asked him or her to track, be it food intake, exercise, or emotions. I always encourage folks to physically write down what I want tracked because just the act of doing so makes the process seem more real and increases the impact. Plans are the same way; physically writing them down demonstrates the importance of the plan to you (and is critical to making adjustments to your plan). Keep your plan visible so that you are reminded of your intentions and (as you check off accomplished sub-goals) your successes. Congratulate yourself on your plan and anticipate success!

While the past sections discussed developing and planning for short- and long-term goals, the next piece addresses learning how to manage your time efficiently and effectively for those goals.

## Capture Time in a Bottle

Time management is such an important topic when it comes to accomplishing your goals that I felt I had to include a brief section on it. If after reading this section, you feel you could benefit from more explicit guidance or instruction, hop on the Internet and Google "time management". You will find more information than you could ever possibly read and learn from.

*What is time management?*

The phrase time management does sound a bit like the butt of a Dilbert cartoon joke, but it is honestly quite important. Time management is simply the act of exercising control over time spent on given activities through use of a set of principles, skills, and tools to improve your quality of life. Naturally, the phrase is usually used with regard to improving productivity, but just getting lots of stuff done isn't the point. Getting useful things done is. Time management can be viewed narrowly, as in what you actually do in terms of physically organizing and scheduling, or much more widely to encompass advance planning and goal setting. Time management also typically includes how to eliminate tasks of less importance.

A key to time management is the list – the task list or the to-do list, it has many names, but I think most of us are familiar with it! Smart people know that there is always more work that can be done. So instead of overwhelming yourself by trying to do it all every single day, you want to be more selective in the allocation of your time and resources. And that's where the to-do list comes in. The to-do list is simply a list of tasks that need completion. You likely can see how this is immediately applicable to the accomplishing of goals. We keep a to-do list to remain organized and to aid our memories. I know I certainly won't remember everything I want to do if I don't write it down. At home I use a white board and at work I use mid-size sticky pads. Both work quite well. If you're more technically minded, you can utilize various types of software on your computer or their equivalents on your smart phone.

Organizing a to-do list can be quite simple – from having a master list of overall goals that you then transfer individual smaller items from the day's to-do list – to seemingly quite complicated. And, of course, there are a bunch in between. For example, you can rank them in order of importance, you can do the easiest ones first, or you can tackle the most unpleasant ones first.

There are three basic keys to the to-do list. First, avoid putting everyday activities on the list, such as eating meals. Second, break down each individual item to the point where the task feels manageable. For example, if your larger goal is to paint your house, what you might put on your daily to-do list is to decide on paint color. The final key, remain flexible and allow for the unexpected. The to-do list is only a helpful guide as much as you allow it to be.

## Practice Exercise – Creating a To-Do List

Based on what I've written above, and considering your daily needs, short-term, and long-term goals, what is on your to-do list for today?

For example, my to-do list for today may have included needed tasks like grocery shopping, along with the short-term task of editing a chapter in my next book that brings me closer to my long-term goal of making my living as a writer. Does your list need adjusting?

Creating a to-do list is important, but as you may have seen in the above practice exercise, there's more to it than just writing down things to do. What follows is a list of concrete suggestions, this time in the form of a question-and-answer for improving your time management. Use what works for you and avoid the poor choices!

## 10 Time Management Questions and Answers

1. Do you keep a to-do list? Failing to keep a to-do list is probably the single biggest mistake you can make in terms of time management. Often times what we're trying to accomplish contains many details that we may struggle to remember without assistance. Take control of your tasks by writing them down.

2. Do you prioritize the items on your to-do list? Not doing this would naturally be the second biggest mistake you can make in terms of time management. Without identifying in advance which tasks are the most important, for example because of their relation to larger goals, you may find yourself easily pulled in multiple other directions not focused on your goals. Prioritize your tasks so that you can focus on the most important ones first and know which really require the most time.

3. Do you set and review your personal goals? Failing to do these will make the first two recommendations on this list worthless. Without knowing your overall direction and the steps that will take

you there, you may feel you're spinning your wheels or you may have difficulty identifying what tasks are important. Keep a list or journal of your personal goals for where you'd like to be in six months, in a year, in five years…whatever span of time seems realistic to accomplish your dreams.

4. Are you productive, or simply busy? Thriving on being busy, whether in pursuit of your goals or not, can lead to increased stress and decreased efficiency as you frantically attempt to complete your tasks for the hour, the day, the week. Instead, if you consider both your normal activities and goal-oriented tasks, you can then plan your time to increase your efficiency and move away from the amped up pace. Take time at the beginning of each week to plan for organizing your schedule.

5. Do you overload yourself with commitments? Taking on too many commitments can be a frequent struggle for people who have a hard time saying no, or who think that unless **they** do it the job won't be done correctly. In either case, when you have too many tasks to do, especially low priority ones for your personal goals, this can result in increased stress and decreased output. Learn to politely say no to activities that are less important and/or learn to delegate and trust others to perform to your standards.

6. Do you schedule activities according to your peak efficiency? Ineffectively scheduling and prioritizing your tasks, activities, and goals may result in poor output, inefficiency, or both. Schedule your most important work for when you feel at your best (right after a workout or when you first wake up, for example) based on your personal history of productivity. In addition, develop and use a time management system in consideration of your personal rhythms to increase your own efficiency and productivity.

7. Do you waste a significant amount of time during the day? Failing to manage bad habits, like being easily distracted or taking on the work of others, wastes more time than most of the items on this list. Luckily it can be relatively easy to fix! Pay attention to what is sucking away your time and begin to minimize those things. Do you spend hours incessantly checking email or Facebook? Then, make a little rule that you won't go online until you've reached the day's goals. Replace each of your identified bad habits with a better habit one at a time until you are as productive as you would like to be.

8. Do you expect perfection before you move on? Being a perfectionist with every single task and working yourself to the bone for fear of losing productivity can be even more problematic than other items on this list because appearing productive and wanting to be perfect come in the guise of goodness. Not all tasks require Herculean effort or perfection. Similarly, not acknowledging that you're human and need down time can result in decreased effectiveness. Notice I didn't say efficiency. To increase effectiveness, recognize what tasks truly need your best effort and ease up on yourself (e.g. take breaks).

9. Do you procrastinate? Beware of procrastination, especially by using unimportant "filler" tasks, to provide excuses or delude yourself into thinking you're progressing. Procrastination frequently occurs because of a feeling of being overwhelmed by the task ahead or by expectations of failure. Approach the items of most importance on your to-do list with an attitude of success and remind yourself that you can always break each of those tasks into smaller ones and start there, building success.

10. Do you proclaim yourself an excellent multitasker? Multitasking is the bane of your existence. Really. I thought I'd end my "mistakes and recommendations" list with this sacred cow. I can't

tell you how many times I've heard someone say how great they are at multitasking, like this is a good thing. No, it's not. Our brains only have so much energy to devote to activity at any one time. If you work on multiple projects, then necessarily you devote less of your brain power to each one than you would if tackled individually, sequentially. Appearing productive by multitasking is not the same as truly being productive. Focus on one important task at a time.

Time management is an area where most people feel like they could always use more help. Hopefully, this brief section provided you with a bump in the right direction. Now let's move on to maintaining the desire to keep moving forward, by discussing motivation (yep, it's so important we're discussing it again, only in greater detail). You can have the best plans, goals, and time management strategies in the world, but without motivation, what good does it do ya?

## Creating and Maintaining Motivation

Put simply, motivation is the "why" behind our actions. It is the explanation for literally everything we do. In this way, it is not something that exists at a single point in time, but rather is a process from start to finish involving biological, emotional, social, and cognitive factors.

Motivation can be either internal or external. Intrinsic (internal) motivation comes from within the individual (e.g., enjoyment of a task itself) and not from any external reward or reinforcement (e.g., payment). Extrinsic (external) motivation is the opposite and comes from outside the individual in the form of some sort of reward or reinforcement. These can be positive consequences (e.g., money, grades) or avoidance of negative consequences (e.g., avoiding punishment). Naturally, it is preferable to develop intrinsic motivation, because then both the process and task itself are more enjoyable and not reliant on a consequence that may not materialize.

Why are you doing what you're doing? When it comes to planning and achieving personal goals, if you don't have a clear reason you are choosing to engage in goal-seeking behavior, you may just be spinning your wheels.

## Practice Exercise – Understanding Motivation

In the last section, I talked about developing goals and explained that a goal is developed to meet a need. Pick one of the goals you've developed, for example, losing 15 pounds. Ask yourself the following questions:

- Why do you want what you're seeking? _____

  _____

  In the example above: To look and feel better.
- Can you visualize attaining your goal? _____

  _____

  In the above example: Picture yourself in a new smaller-sized outfit.
- What are options for attaining your goal? _____

  _____

  In the example above: reduce calories consumed and/or exercise more.
- What do you enjoy that can help?_____

  _____

  In the example above: Being social – join a hiking club.

Consider your past and visualize your future. Now move forward! With that in mind, here are specific recommendations that may help you along your path.

## 9 Motivational Recommendations

1. Know and understand your big goal. Do you know where you're going? Have you broken your primary goal down into smaller, manageable bites? It's easier to motivate yourself to continue a marathon if you can both see the finish line and build confidence with each successfully completed mile!

2. Avoid procrastination, accept unwanted outcomes, and finish what you start. These may seem like separate ideas, but they're interconnected. If you don't start, you can't finish successfully. All successful people know that failure occurs on the path to success. And always move forward toward that finish line (or the next start line, since really this is all a life process anyway!)

3. Believe that you will be successful, but remember that some things are outside of your control or require time to develop and that you need to reward your effort as well as success. By focusing on effort over outcome, you develop intrinsic motivation to continue the behavior until the outcome you want arrives.

4. Recognize when something can be accomplished routinely and when you need to engage self-discipline. For example, if you don't particularly enjoy checking email, you can set a specific time to do it, get in the habit of checking only then, and forget about it the rest of the time.

5. Modify your thoughts (as discussed in *Step 4*) to make an unpleasant task enjoyable, associate pleasure with the unpleasant task (listening to music while you check email), or finally, if necessary, recognize that you may have to endure some pain now for the results you want later (exercising can be the perfect literal example).

6. Keep your enthusiasm (and thus your motivation) at its highest levels by consistently reaffirming your belief in your activities. This may involve thinking about your interests, joining groups to associate with others who share your interests, or simply reading about your interests. Without enthusiasm, interest begins to flag and activity becomes drudgery. Isn't the point of this entire book to increase your happiness?

7. Do something! This may seem overly simplistic, but my procrastinating readers know that once you stop moving, it becomes easier to remain stopped. It's the science of inertia. On the other hand, science also says a body in motion stays in motion. Stay in motion. As you continue to move forward you'll find increasing inspiration to keep putting in the effort.

8. Find someone with similar goals who complements your strengths with their own strengths. Together, you can buoy each other up when necessary, learn from each other, and share your positive approaches and attitude. This can be especially helpful related to solitary tasks. For example, an author can join a writing group and partner up with a fellow writer, not necessarily to co-author anything, but to assist each other in maintaining motivation.

9. Visualize your goals with happiness by making them meaningful from the beginning. Know your ultimate purpose in developing your goals and keep them relevant by constantly reassessing. If you find that your values have shifted, it's okay to change your goals to fit who you are today. See yourself happily attaining these new goals. Sometimes it can be helpful to take pictures or cut photos out of magazines – or even draw pictures yourself! – of representations of your goals.

## Practice Exercise – Maintaining Motivation

Consider what has stymied your progress in the past and what helped you overcome it:
1. E.g., Procrastination / overcome it by prioritizing my to-do list
2. Fear of failure / overcome it by considering my past successes
3. _____
4. _____

Consider what may stymie progress toward your identified long-term goal of _____ (e.g., a million dollars in the bank):
1. E.g., Unexpected expenses / overcome this by putting $50/month into an emergency fund
2. Feeling deprived / overcome this by reviewing reasons for goal, modifying if necessary, and considering benefits of goal
3. _____
_____
4. _____
_____

If a goal is important, motivation will propel you toward success. By having a clear and compelling vision of what you want to achieve, you can use motivation to strengthen your desire, increase initiative, and maintain persistence along your path. Remember that everyone struggles with low motivation sometimes, but if you need to motivate yourself constantly, you may want to take a hard look at your identified goals to make sure they're **your** goals and not what your parents, spouse, friends, or society thinks you **should** be achieving.

# Vignette

Sam plopped onto my couch and expressed that he needed to make a life change. I asked him to elaborate and he proceeded to articulate that he had been unhappy in his job for quite some time and he wanted to go back to school for an advanced degree in business. Unfortunately that was as far as he had gotten! He came to see me for my assistance in making that dream a reality.

The first thing we did was explore the essential reasons why Sam did not like his job. He worked in finance directly with the customers but he wanted to move higher up the corporate ladder and have more responsibility (and make more money). I asked him how having an advanced business degree would help – in other words, how did this become his plan/long-term goal? He explained that at his last work evaluation, he had been explicitly told that he would not be promoted much higher without the advanced degree.

Okay, so Sam had a five year plan of being promoted to a specific position within his company. Through his current supervisor he learned that he could not achieve that plan without an advanced degree. Thus, earning that degree became his 2-3 year long-term goal. Sam was off to a pretty good start, because he knew exactly why he was creating his plan and he had very specific long-term goals. What he needed from me was help to develop the short-term goals and relevant plan that would take him there.

Sam's specific goal that he and I would be planning together was to identify an appropriate graduate school that he would be accepted in to. The first thing we did was work out exactly when he wanted to begin graduate school. He intended to start the next fall, meaning that he would be a part of that spring's application process. Armed with that knowledge, we began to structure his new plan.

Sam knew he needed to have his application in to his possible schools by the spring, so that gave him an absolute deadline for all of his goal activity. Working backward, he identified that he needed to begin now if he was going to make that deadline. We started with his first task of identifying what school he wanted to go to. Sam's short-term goals became: researching available schools, identifying ones to apply to, determining what he needed for the applications, and then actually collecting and submitting all of the necessary pieces.

Together, Sam and I developed even shorter-term goals for each of his identified short-term goals for his long-term goal of earning a graduate degree. As an example, once he identified the two schools with degree programs of interest in his geographic location and reviewed their application requirements online, together we created a plan for meeting those requirements. He developed a to-do list of all of the application items (entrance test, references, application form, undergraduate transcripts, and application fee). Then he developed individual to-do lists related to the items as he pursued them. As he accomplished each item on the to-do lists, he crossed it off.

By organizing his approach and noting his successes as he moved forward, he remained motivated. With each step, he became more excited about moving in this new direction. When he found himself occasionally feeling overwhelmed by the minutia of the process, he would visualize himself walking across that stage with his cap and gown. He also found my available support invaluable as a cheerleader and coach, even though I wasn't going through the same process.

By following the guidance offered in this section, Sam was able to successfully break down his long-term goal of promotion into other goals, including obtaining a graduate degree, and then breaking that down into the short-term goal of being accepted into an advanced degree program and working on that goal explicitly – with the ultimate result that he was accepted into the graduate school of his choice!

## Chapter Purpose

Obtaining your goals takes planning. The purpose of this chapter was to assist you in identifying your goals, both long-term and short-term, by finding solutions to problems to create your ideal life. You could then determine how best to plan for achieving them, and ways to help yourself maintain motivation during the inevitable tougher times.

## Practice Exercise Checklist

- Imagining Your Ideal Life – Trying to identify goals, especially long-term goals, can be daunting, so this first practice exercise asks you to consider what your ideal life would look like and what some potential long-term goals could be developed from that idea.

- Short-Term Goals – Since long-term goals likely consist of large goals, and probably multi-step goals, this is where short-term goals come in. Identify short-term goals related to your long-term goal(s).

- Identifying Parts of Your Goal – Using your answers to the above practice exercises, begin the intellectual process of moving from identifying the problem in your life you're looking to solve, breaking it down into its pieces, and visualizing what it would look like to solve.

- Creating a To-Do List – Moving from developing goals to actually accomplishing them, consider the most powerful tool of them all – the to-do list. Write down the items on today's list, making certain that there are items related to your short- and long-term goals, in addition to unrelated but necessary needs.

- Understanding Motivation – Pick a goal and then ask yourself questions about your motivation for attaining that goal. Include visualizing the goal, options for attaining the goal, and activities you enjoy that may help you toward your goal.

- Maintaining Motivation – The final practice exercise of the chapter has two pieces. One, consider what has caused your motivation to flag in the past and what you did to overcome that. Two, consider what may cause your motivation to lapse while pursuing your current goal and some options that may help to overcome them.

Now that you've actively considered how you think about yourself and the world, and considered how to plan for what you want, now it's time to move beyond ourselves and consider our role in the world.

# Part 3
# SPIRIT

## STEP 7
## COMMUNITY

*An individual has not started living until he can rise above the narrow confines of his individualistic concerns to the broader concerns of all humanity.*
Martin Luther King, Jr. (Civil Rights Activist)

I'm choosing to begin this particular *Step* by returning to a familiar topic, positive psychology. This only makes sense, since the concepts of positive psychology have always felt so personally resonant and, indeed, partially were the inspiration to write a self-help book at all. Plus, when we talk about moving beyond ourselves, as this *Step* at its core will be asking you to do, beginning with the meaningful life as presented by Martin Seligman and positive psychology is a pretty good way to begin.

### What is the Meaningful Life?

The meaningful life in positive psychology consists of using one's strengths and talents to belong to and serve something that one believes is bigger than the self. This explains the subtitle, if you will, of the meaningful life, which is the life of affiliation. The meaningful life concerns how individuals derive a positive sense of wellbeing (happiness!), belonging, meaning, and purpose from being part of and contributing back to something larger and more permanent than themselves. In short, the meaningful life involves participation in activities outside of the self, for the good of society.

*What is outside of yourself?*

You may wonder what exactly is meant by something larger and more permanent than ourselves. Well, it means just about anything. It can be as grand and seemingly permanent as nature itself. It can be as small and intimate as your immediate family. And, it can be everything in between. Any organization – social group, church, military – has the potential to fit the bill. Additionally, any movement, tradition, or belief system also can be considered an institution larger than yourself.

There are thus many ways to participate in activities outside of yourself. Every time you sit down to family dinner, you are contributing to your meaningful life. Every time you coach your daughter's soccer team, you are contributing to your meaningful life. Every time you write a letter to your Senator, you are contributing to your meaningful life. Hopefully, you can see that the ways in which you can move outside of yourself and give back to your community are practically endless!

## Societal Good

If the meaningful life is developed through participation in activities outside of the self, for the good of society, how are the examples I just provided for the good of society? That's an excellent question! To begin, an argument can be made that any connection to another could be considered for the good of society because it is through such connections that we desire to protect and love one another within any larger societal groups.

By sitting down to dinner every night with your family, for example, you are supporting and advancing your family unit. Your family is like a mini-society. Strengthening your family cohesiveness can only help improve the connection, functioning, and wellbeing of the larger society. You can see this through the involvement of your family with: your children's schools, the community watch program, and the neighborhood block party, to name just a few possibilities.

The ultimate key to this entire idea is that everyone is connected. Supporting each other, and using your strengths to improve and increase that support within the smallest societal units, like the family unit, can have a huge cumulative positive impact on every other societal unit, from the community to world-wide.

*What is community?*

Maybe you're wondering just what I mean by community. I keep throwing the word around willy-nilly. The primary meaning of community describes the configuration of the individuals themselves. Thus, a community is a group of interacting people, generally larger than a single household, living in the same geographical area, typically sharing common values, operating under the same laws and government. The term community also references the area itself in which the group resides. So, community can refer both to the people in a particular area and the area itself.

Community can also refer to a group of folks with something specific in common. For example, a group, irrespective of geography, who share a common interest, can be called a community (e.g., the scientific community). Or, a group, also irrespective of geography, that forms a specific segment of society, can be a community (e.g., the Latino community). In these instances, there is still the expectation of a natural sense of affiliation and common beliefs based on membership in the community.

As an offshoot of the idea of sharing a common interest, community can also refer to sharing *identity* itself, or just the act of sharing or fellowship. For example, when we feel a connection or affiliation within a group of any size, we may describe feeling a sense of community.

And, finally, community can refer to society as a whole. It can refer to the national or international community; essentially the public itself. The media especially will employ the term community in this way.

Oh, wait, that's not quite it! There's one more use of the term community that completely obliterates the idea of geographical proximity within community, and that's in reference to the Internet. Yes, technically, this use of the term falls under the second paragraph above, but the Internet so fundamentally altered the idea and expression of community that it bears special mention. Now, anyone with any interest can find a group of like-minded individuals. Whether or not one agrees with the belief that the Internet has had a negative impact on physical community, one cannot deny the increase in electronic affiliation that has resulted as well.

## Why is it Necessary to Belong?

That may seem like an odd question. Our instinct is that of course it's necessary to belong to something bigger than yourself. But, why? And what exactly is belonging anyway? Let me take a few moments to explore exactly what defines a sense of belonging, and why we do it, before we delve into ways to make that happen.

A sense of belonging is the feeling of being connected with others. It involves feeling secure in our positions, recognized within our groups, and able to participate to feel a part of society. A sense of belonging is naturally interrelated with how much you participate in society – the more you participate, the more you feel connected, the more you participate, and so on. Clearly, feeling like you belong would positively influence your sense of identity. Feeling like you belong somewhere, like you fit in, is important from early childhood, and helps to improve physical and mental health across the lifespan, reducing childhood and adolescent behavior problems, as well as adult mood symptoms.

## We want and need to be part of a group because it is value-added – it gives more meaning to our life.

Part of how a sense of belonging can provide more meaning is that it helps your sense of identity and boosts your feelings of self-worth. Though ideally these are additions to, and not reliant solely on, external factors. We feel wanted and loved when we are part of a group larger than ourselves. When we believe we are wanted and loved, we feel better about ourselves individually. This comes in part from the sense of identity that belonging to different groups provides. As a fun example, think about how affiliated people are to their specific sports teams. I, for example, am a huge Miami Dolphins and New York Giants football fan (gotta have a team in the AFC and NFC!), and I feel an immediate kinship with a perfect stranger who professes a similar allegiance.

Being a member of a group allows us to draw strength from the life experiences, opinions, and advice of others within our group. Especially if the members of your own group share your opinions and beliefs, this can help you to express yourself. Such a sense of belonging can be critical for more marginalized groups in society – for example, gay, lesbian, bisexual, and transgendered adolescents may rely heavily on group membership to feel safe and secure in being themselves.

A sense of belonging to a group can actually help guide you with life decisions, such as educational and career achievement. While you don't want to get caught up in "keeping up with the Jones's" (especially in terms of material wealth), group desires and achievement can guide you within your own life. Remember that this can be a positive or a negative. A negative example could be that if your coworkers emphasize doing only the minimum, you may be less inclined to "outshine" them for fear of being ostracized from the group. A positive example could be if your coworkers value continuing education and support your efforts as well.

Finally, humans like to define, group, and categorize everything in life. We love our labels! Our own membership in a group, and knowing others are a part of a specific group, helps us each to understand the other better. Although the assumptions we make may be incorrect, which is where negative stereotyping comes from, the fact is that knowing someone is a college graduate, a military member, or a politician gives us a place to start in feeling like we know at least a piece of who they are.

As you can hopefully see, there are many reasons why we seek to belong, why we seek that sense of being part of something larger than ourselves. It is helpful to us, to each other, and to society as a whole. Frankly, it's basically a biological and psychological imperative that we seek to belong. Given all of that, let's turn our thoughts now to how we can achieve an increased sense of belonging.

## Committing to Improving Belonging

Let's take a much more explicit look at what involvement in something bigger than yourself means. Obviously, each individual person will have his or her own unique interpretation and application of the phrase, but moving through the different societal units of "something bigger than yourself" may be helpful to put concrete ideas and examples out there for you to see what resonates personally.

## We are Family

Clearly, the smallest societal unit outside of yourself is the family. This can be as basic as a spouse or life partner, or as complicated as a blended family with a dozen biological, step-, and adopted children. The exact configuration is irrelevant, of course. The concepts and suggestions apply, regardless. For my single readers out there, family can also include good friends and children of the furry persuasion!

And, family may certainly include your family of origin, or the people you grew up with.

## Practice Exercise – Friends and Family Connections

Who makes up your innermost circle? Who are your friends and family that you feel most connected to?

1. E.g., Spouse
2. _____
3. _____
4. _____

In the above examples, what's the last activity you did with each of those connections? Or the last contact with them, if they live in another town? In my example of spouse, our last activity was hiking. Write down the activities next to the entries above and if you have to go back a bit, this lets you know this is an area you can develop.

Within the family, there are both small and big things that you can do to increase your sense of belonging. Remember that none of these are groundbreaking ideas, but it may take effort to engage in them if you have not been doing so previously.

*Every little bit counts*

Several small examples include, having dinner together every night, or at least on more nights than not, in order to maintain comfortable connection; designating a weekly date or family night, or both, allowing time to reconnect through relaxed fun; and, especially if you're long-distance, emailing on a regular basis, or even better, mailing a letter or picking up the phone just-because, as opposed to waiting for a "reason".

*Sometimes bigger is better*

A few mid-size examples include, celebrating important personal occasions or milestones, like birthdays, anniversaries, and placing first at the high school track meet; celebrating major cultural events within the family structure, like national holidays and religious rites of passage.

*Let's show 'em what you got!*

Finally, a couple of large, likely to be more infrequent, examples include taking major vacations, like a European cruise or a trip to Disney World, or if you're from a more adventurous clan, choosing to move to a new city to start fresh (this one is popular with me!)

# Neighborhood

When I write neighborhood, I mean the immediate area where you live. In smaller towns, this may not seem as relevant as in larger cities, but of course it is. And, it's critical if you live in a larger city just because of the sheer numbers of people we're talking about. Thus, when I speak of neighborhood, I'm mostly talking about the block or two around your immediate home. Much larger than that and you're talking town at that point, which is the next level.

## Practice Exercise – Neighborhood Connections

How involved are you in your neighborhood? What activities have you engaged in?

1. E.g., Know my neighbors' names
2. _____
3. _____
4. _____

There are tons of ways you can get more involved within your neighborhood. In our increasingly insular world, we may find it correspondingly increasingly difficult to remain involved in our neighborhoods. I can't tell you how many people who live in apartment complexes don't even know their neighbors' names!

*Small action, big impact*

Smaller activities you can engage in are to simply learn who your neighbors are. Knock on some doors and introduce yourself to the folks who live around you. Make a concerted effort to spend more time outside to increase random encounters with neighbors, which will offer a brief chance to engage in conversation on a regular basis. Other easy ideas require minor planning, such as checking on a neighbor's house when they're out of town or babysitting for a couple so they can have a date night.

*Let's have a party!*

There are also larger activities that require even more coordination, such as hosting neighborhood block parties where everyone comes out for food and company. Or organizing a neighborhood watch, which fosters togetherness while also protecting each other. That's definitely a win-win!

## City/Town

One level up from the neighborhood is clearly the town or city in which you reside. Or you may feel like you a have a town within a city – what I mean is that some cities are so large, there may actually be two levels here – portions of the larger city as well as the city itself. For example, you may live in the city of Los Angeles and apply these suggestions to both that larger city as well as the smaller town-like subdivision in which you actually reside, such as Santa Monica.

## Practice Exercise – City/Town Connections

Do you feel connected to your city or town? What involvement do you have in your town or city?

1. E.g., Running club
2. _____
3. _____
4. _____

*Groups everywhere*

One of the easiest ways to become part of your city or town is to identify activities you enjoy and find groups of like-minded people. Your only limit is your imagination. There are groups for almost everything. This can include, for example, community theater, citizens' police academy, or toast masters. As someone who has moved many times as an adult, I can attest to the ease with which these groups can be joined. In fact, I've done all three of the ones I listed above. A great resource for this that I mentioned in an early chapter is meetup.com; on this free website, you enter your city and activities you're interested in – and voila, a list of groups pops up.

You can also check out the city's website and look for a community calendar of events that will list upcoming activities. Try to engage in events that are unique to your area. For example, when I lived in Wichita Falls, Texas, I participated in a bicycle event known as Hotter-n-Hell Hundred. Participation in this historic event allowed me the opportunity to do something I enjoyed, along with thousands of like-minded individuals from around the country (even the world), while being a part of my community. There are, of course, smaller athletic events, like 5K run/walks for various charitable endeavors.

*Actually giving back*

Speaking of charity, one great option is to become involved in activities that directly give back (and I'll speak more extensively about volunteering in the next section), like helping to build homes for Habitat for Humanity, or volunteering your time to walk dogs or socialize cats at the local humane society shelter. You can also support local businesses and frequent their establishments as often as you visit the big box stores. Finally, one way to become involved in the workings of your city or town is to become involved politically.

## State and National

As you consider the next larger societal group from the city level, you reach the state. I don't really have to define what I mean by this level; there are handy lines that delineate one state from another, right? I've lived in eight states and I'm always entertained by how enthusiastically loyal individuals from certain states are. Just remember it can be a fine line between support for your state and dogmatically excluding everyone else. Be supportive without setting up a zero-sum game of us-versus-them. That's the goal.

Much like at the state level, the national level is also fairly well defined. I am aware that some of those lines are…fuzzy…and that some nations come and go, or are still trying to get recognition. This is not the time or place for political debate, so I'll stick with a simple description – a nation is defined by its people, customs, and cultures, but is generally marked on a map by a line from the countries surrounding it.

## Practice Exercise – State and National Connections

How connected are you at the state and national levels? Can you identify any affiliation at this level?

1. E.g., American Red Cross volunteer
2. _____
3. _____
4. _____

*Politics doesn't have to be a bad word*

What can you, a single individual, do to be more involved at the state or national levels? To piggyback off the last section, political involvement is always a huge option. This can be fairly simple and basic – you wouldn't even have to leave your home! You can email, mail, or call your state representatives, such as the state senators or governor. This serves dual purposes. You can be more physically involved, plus you'll have a sense of being heard. A slightly more involved idea is to volunteer for a state or national political campaign (and you can do this at a lower level too). This would get you out and about in your own neighborhood, city, or town, as well as possibly offer the opportunity for more state or national involvement. A considerably more active option is to run for an office yourself! Now you may not be able to just jump right in and run for office, but maybe that can be a goal?

Other options can include supporting your state's flagship universities, either financially or with your time, through donations, volunteering, or attending their athletic and cultural events. Another option is to join state level groups, for example, emergency response groups. I thought of this one because, as a psychologist, when I lived in the state of New York, I learned of a group for medical professionals. Although I moved away before I had the opportunity to join, I could have registered with the group and been available in the case of a state emergency, such as following a flood. Go online to see what your state has available, or start with a national group and work your way down to the state level.

As you consider community involvement on a larger scale it can seem more daunting. Disaster response is one area where states and nations typically come together. I'll therefore start with that, but keep in mind that you don't want death and destruction to become the only times we come together.

There are national disasters, like 9/11 or Hurricane Katrina, that are immediate, vivid, and heartbreaking. Listening for requests for assistance and then responding is an excellent way of being involved in something larger than yourself on a national level. But, remember there are also opportunities to help with less attention-grabbing national disasters.

Anyone who knows me, knows that animal welfare is the cause probably nearest to my heart. As of this writing, there are still 3-5 million animals who are killed in shelters every year. I mention this to explain that this national disaster is a perfect opportunity to help. National organizations work to move animals from kill shelters to no-kill shelters, frequently across state lines. Best Friends Animal Society's Pup My Ride is the perfect example. Through a network of linked individuals, puppies and dogs are moved across the country from kill shelters to either no-kill shelters or to forever homes. This is just one of many examples of how you can get involved at the national level.

## Citizen of the World

We now reach the highest societal level, the world. I have no pithy definition for what I mean – the world is simply the world - everything we share on this rock we call Earth. Insularity within your own country is the biggest cause of an us-versus-them attitude. The only way to truly become a citizen of the world is to realize that borders are ultimately artificial constructs. I urge you to be aware of the world's issues to see where you can participate.

As at all the preceding societal levels, there are opportunities to get involved at the world level. At the small end of the spectrum, which you can do in your pajamas sitting at your computer, are any number of online examples. You can create, sign, and share online petitions about issues of concern, such as the intention of a government in another country to stone a pregnant woman to death for adultery. You can also become involved in fundraising efforts for organizations attempting to help war-ravaged countries, or those hit with natural disasters, like typhoons. You can draft emails, share information with friends and family, and just generally assist with the electronic end of any number of international volunteer efforts.

In the mid-range, you can put both your money and your time where your mouth is by physically volunteering for short periods in other countries. There are groups who arrange eco-tours, research groups, and volunteer expeditions for the short-term, such as Earthwatch and Global Vision International. If you're feeling really adventurous, you can go all in and make a big investment in another country by working with an organization like the Peace Corps.

## To Give a Little, or a Lot

Clearly a primary theme as you read through that last section, and what one generally thinks of when they think of belonging and community, is the idea of volunteering. I'm therefore going to spend a moment longer and give a special mention of volunteering as vitally important to developing meaning in your life.

*What is volunteering?*

One definition that I've seen for volunteering is stepping outside of ourselves and doing something for the benefit of another without an expectation of gaining something in return. To quote The

Canadian Code for Volunteer Involvement (2006, found online), "Volunteering is the most fundamental act of citizenship and philanthropy in our society. It is offering time, energy, and skills of one's own free will."

Volunteering adds to the creation of a true community. When you work to improve your home and life, your neighbor's home and life, a stranger's home and life, you change lives and decrease suffering throughout the area. As you choose to help others, you also likely gain skills, self-esteem, and goodwill.

Volunteering, therefore, isn't selfless, because clearly we each gain something from engaging in the behavior. This isn't a bad thing. This is what we call a win-win situation. Volunteering has all of the benefits above for yourself, the individual you're helping, the community as a whole, and in essence, the world. How cool is that?

## Helpful Hint

While any volunteering is good volunteering, matching the volunteering to your own personal values, strengths, and interests will intensify your desire to volunteer initially and maintain volunteering when the blush of excitement at the start possibly wears off. In addition, through this matching, it enhances your own personal benefits from volunteering.

## Practice Exercise – Volunteer Assessment

Keeping in mind our definition above of volunteering, this can be big or small. Do you volunteer now? If so, doing what?

1. E.g., Mow neighbor's lawn
2. Deliver food to the homebound
3. _____
4. _____

If you do not currently volunteer, why not? What are your barriers?

1. E.g., Time
2. Transportation
3. _____
4. _____

Consider what you wrote above and problem solve. For example, if time is an issue, remember what I wrote in an earlier chapter – we all have the same 24 hours in a day. Choose to prioritize giving back, even if it's just once a month.

Matching your volunteering to your personal values, strengths, and interests can be accomplished any number of ways. Think about your own personal values first. I briefly got on my soapbox earlier when discussing animal welfare. I know that loving, caring for, and protecting animals are important to me. Therefore, when looking to volunteer, I could consider that first. I chose to volunteer at the local humane society. What's important to you? Children? Then consider volunteering for a mentoring program or reading to children at the library. Nature? Then consider volunteering to be a tour guide at a local nature preserve.

Think about your own strengths. What are you good at, especially skills that others may not possess? Earlier I mentioned Habitat for Humanity. If you're handy with a hammer and screwdriver, volunteering to help build homes could be a perfect match to your particular skill set. If you're good at computers, perhaps you could volunteer to teach senior citizens the basics of how to operate and navigate a computer.

Think about your interests. If you love to sing and dance, consider volunteering to work at your local theater, either onstage or backstage. Or volunteering at the local YMCA. If you're interested in the arts, volunteer to work with the homeless in art classes. If you're a musician, consider a program to play for children with cancer in the hospital. Whatever you like to do, there is someone who could benefit from your interest and enthusiasm.

*How do you find where to volunteer?*

This seems to be a big obstacle for folks. My clients almost all express a willingness and desire to try volunteering, however they often stumble out of the gate because they don't have any idea how to find where to go. My response is pretty simple. Gotta love the Internet! There are national and local websites that exist solely to present volunteer opportunities to interested individuals. For example, I used volunteermatch.org to find a public affairs volunteer position with the American Red Cross. You can also Google "volunteer" with your city name to find a plethora of possibilities.

Another option is to ask friends and family where they volunteer – and if they don't, maybe you guys can find something together! The buddy system is as great for volunteering as it is for working out. A final option is to simply call an organization that you're interested in and ask if they would like a volunteer. Many places would love to have someone willing to help out for free and would jump at the chance to have you.

## Practice Exercise – Identifying Volunteer Opportunities

Based on the above, I'd like you to identify three possibilities for volunteering. Writing them down doesn't mean you'll do all three, but it's a place for you to start doing additional research.

1. _____
2. _____
3. _____

Based on your list, pick one to start with and actually volunteer for them. If it's a good fit, wonderful. If it's not, try one of the remaining two options you identified. As you experiment with these volunteer activities, whether they are each a good fit or not, you're gathering valuable information about what your preferences are and are not.

> Remember that regardless of your life circumstances, you have the power to give the gift of time.

## Vignette

Nick arrived in my office appearing somewhat unsure why he was even there. He immediately told me that he had made the appointment because he felt that something was off about his life. He was having difficulty pinpointing what the problem was, and so was unable to fix it himself. He made the appointment to obtain clarity about his situation, as well as direct assistance and guidance in solving whatever these unknown problems were.

In exploring Nick's current functioning, I learned that he was a married, childless man, living far from his family of origin. He graduated from college and worked in an engineering firm. He loved his wife, loved his job, and generally felt happy, but there was a dissatisfaction that he was unable to pinpoint. After working through some thought modification for a couple of weeks, Nick saw substantial improvement. However, there was still a niggling of doubt; there was still a feeling like there was more.

Nick was interested in the concept of belonging and finding meaning in his life outside of himself. He had spent a great deal of time in his life and therapy focused on himself and he quickly responded to the suggestion of looking beyond himself. Together, we decided to explore his affiliation with others in his life, from his immediate social circles to the entire world around him.

Beginning with his most important and intimate relationship, we discussed his wife and the ups and downs. They had been married for ten years and were still very much in love. Nick came to realize, though, that they were not as active together as they once were and he missed that. His homework then was to speak with his wife about how she was feeling. She surprised him by stating that she had been feeling the exact same way for a while but hadn't been sure how to broach the topic since he seemed so content with the status quo. They made a commitment to start with a weekly date night.

Beyond his wife, when Nick thought about his family, he soon realized that he missed them. He had moved far away from his original home and only saw or spoke to his family on birthdays or major holidays. There was little regular interaction. Nick saw that there were quick fixes to this and set up reminders on his phone to call his parents and his sister every weekend. Although they were at first surprised by the sudden unexpected increase in contact, they later told him how much they had missed him too and were appreciative of the effort to improve communication.

Moving on to his friends and the community, Nick decided things were pretty good with his friends. He saw one or more of them at least every week, hanging out to watch a sporting event, and that felt satisfying and secure. When he thought about his involvement within his community, he decided there was definitely more he could do. He looked into volunteering at the local community center, helping out wherever they needed it and working with the adolescents and their families. Nick felt that he was using his strengths to potentially improve the lives of folks directly in his community.

Nick explored the ideas of increasing involvement at the city and state levels, and ultimately decided that his current level of involvement (donating to political candidates he supported and occasionally placing calls to them) was sufficient. At the national and international levels, however, he recognized that he was doing nothing to be involved in this larger world. So, he made it a priority to stay abreast of political and cultural information. He implemented this by scanning the newspapers (well, websites of newspapers!) of other countries to both learn what were the issues of the day for them, but also how the US issues were being reported elsewhere. Through this, he decided to join Amnesty International and become active in their campaigns.

After several months of analyzing and increasing his involvement in activities relating to people and institutions outside of himself (as well as the initial cognitive therapy), Nick successfully increased his sense of belonging in the world around him, big and small.

## Chapter Purpose

How connected do you feel to the world outside of yourself? The purpose of *Step 7* was to get you to think about your connections, from family through international. Many of these areas may just need tweaking, whereas others are completely neglected. I closed the chapter with a strong recommendation to consider volunteering as an excellent way to increase connections with others.

## Practice Exercise Checklist

- Friends and Family Connections – Outside of ourselves, the first connections to consider and strengthen are with your friends and family. Consider who your closest friends and family are and, importantly, how much interaction you actually have with them.

- Neighborhood Connections – Then move up a societal level to consider how involved you are in your neighborhood. To make a neighborhood more than just a collection of houses, this type of involvement can be critical, even if it's just learning your neighbors' names.

- City/Town Connections – Moving up another societal level, consider your involvement within your city or town. Are you able to identify anything? The higher up the levels we go, typically the more challenging it is to identify connections.

- State and National Connections – People rarely consider their involvement at the state or national societal levels (let alone the international level), so this practice exercise asks you to consider ways in which you currently are connected at these levels. As with the other levels, if you find yourself struggling, consider the suggestions made for increasing connections.

- Volunteer Assessment – Volunteering is beneficial for ourselves and our community. This practice exercise asks you to consider what volunteering you currently do, big and small, structured or unstructured. If you aren't currently volunteering, the follow-up is to identify the barriers and begin to problem solve.

- Identifying Volunteer Opportunities – The final practice exercise of the chapter asks you to brainstorm three possibilities for volunteering, not with the expectation that you'll necessarily do all of them, but as a place to start for identifying at least one that you can do regularly.

Volunteering is one great way to look outside of oneself to see the world as a huge amazing place. Doing things for others is an excellent way to increase our own happiness. Next, in *Step 8,* I'll discuss spirituality and mindfulness as other ways to increase our happiness by looking outside of our narrow interests and considering who and what is most important to us.

# STEP 8
# SPIRITUALITY & MINDFULNESS

*Too many people spend money they haven't earned, to buy things they don't want, to impress people they don't like.*
Will Rogers (American humorist)

This chapter is essentially a catchall category of interconnected ideas: spirituality, mindfulness, minimalism, and gratitude. I present them together in this chapter precisely because they naturally fit together. If they don't seem to for you yet, trust that by the end of the chapter, they will! Follow along as I walk through each of these topics.

## Spirituality

Even beyond just an overall sense of community, some kind of spirituality is vital to happiness. When discussing spirituality, we immediately find that there are many different beliefs encompassed by the word. There is both religious spirituality and secular spirituality. The significant difference between them is that for someone who considers themselves religious, their spirituality is bound within a specific faith tradition that includes, most often, belief in a higher power traditionally defined as an omnipresent, omnipotent, and omniscient being.

*Secular spirituality*

Increasingly people describe themselves as spiritual but not religious. They recognize there are many spiritual paths, not all of which are from traditional religious faiths. Spirituality emphasizes moving beyond a materialistic view of the world, focusing on the transcendent nature of the world, without (necessarily) accepting a belief in a supernatural reality or a divine being (God). In other words, people who describe themselves as spiritual but not religious often state that they believe in a power greater than themselves but typically it is not an all-knowing, ever-present, God-like being.

Spirituality can represent a path to your innermost values and beliefs. It also can reflect a sense of interconnectedness with a larger reality, such as all living creatures, and that everyone within that reality is mutually dependent on the other. By possessing an awareness of your purpose and overall meaning of life, your spirituality can assist you in identifying your deepest, absolute values. Ideally, these beliefs can be a source of inspiration for you as you find meaning and inner peace in your life. Qualities such as compassion, love, forgiveness, harmony, tolerance, and concern for others are frequently cited as spiritual qualities.

*Why is spirituality helpful?*

For health and happiness! As mental health and physical health are flip sides of the same coin, you can't have full health in one without addressing the other. I've seen that repeated time and again with my patients and clients. What does that look like in the context of spirituality?

# Happiness

Spirituality directly contributes to increased happiness through the development of optimism, hope, and forgiveness. By fostering feelings of optimism and hope, and subsequently through improved coping skills, spirituality reduces sadness and worry. Forgiveness releases hostility and resentment for past actions and, by doing so, can reduce anger, increase hopefulness, and enable individuals to better manage all emotions. Finally, having a well-developed social support network of family and friends lends itself to less experienced stress and increased contentedness. Spirituality and spiritual practices encourage overall relaxation with the result that you simply feel better emotionally.

## Health

Those same concepts that decrease negative emotions and increase positive ones are related to overall physical health. Having hope, or a positive attitude in the face of adversity, is linked to fewer illnesses over the course of your life. Forgiving yourself and believing a higher power has forgiven you may help to reduce feelings like anger and resentment. In addition, faith in something positive may directly influence health by increasing belief in your ability to achieve and maintain healthiness.

*How can you develop spirituality?*

Spiritual practices are essential for personal health as you search for inner peace and happiness. They are intended to develop your inner life, to assist you with manifestation of positive humanistic concepts and connection to something larger than yourself. They help you foster a connection to a supernatural being if you have a belief in one, but also help you manage thoughts and emotions that can be inhibiting or expanding in your development of inner peace and satisfaction. Spiritual practices include general practices like mindfulness and contemplation, as well as more active practices like meditation and prayer.

## Spiritual Beliefs

I considered discussing a number of traditional and nontraditional religious/spiritual beliefs but ultimately decided that level of detail was outside the scope of this book and better left to individual consideration. What I will write is that if you feel that a faith other than your currently practiced one sounds appealing, or perhaps a better match, then by all means do some additional research and explore. You may find something resonates better with you for a reason.

*What are some of the more common spiritual beliefs?*
There are many non-traditional, traditional, and monotheistic spiritual/religious beliefs. Definitions naturally vary, but when I speak of non-traditional spiritual beliefs, I am referring to belief systems that are not your standard practiced in Western societies. Possibilities include: paganism, Native American beliefs, and Wiccan. As we move into more traditional spiritual beliefs, Buddhism and Hinduism are clear examples. And, finally, the most popular monotheistic religions are Judaism, Christianity, and Islam.

## Practice Exercise – Spiritual Identification

Depending on your degree of spiritual identification already, you may wish to do more or less of the following practice exercise. At the very least, you'll want to consider #1 below:

1. Identify your own personal spiritual or religious beliefs. Remember that just because you were raised in a particular tradition, or because you've "always" been in a certain column, doesn't mean you have to stay there. Ask yourself if you feel fulfilled in your faith. If the answer is "no" or "I don't know", there are two options:
    a. Speak with someone you trust within your faith and explore

your lack of fulfillment. Determine when your faith began decreasing; consider if something happened to shake your faith that maybe could be overcome. If you are able to reignite your belief in your current faith, that's great. You can jump to #3 below. If not, continue to option b.

b. If you are unable to reignite your belief in your current faith, or after reflection have decided it simply is not a good fit, I encourage you to spend time considering alternatives.

2. After identifying what calls to you, if you have decided that you would like to go in a new faith direction, the next step is to do more research. This may involve reviewing websites on the Internet, reading books about the beliefs in which you have an interest, and most importantly, speaking to people who already ascribe to the faith. Make every effort to find someone local with whom you can sit down and just talk. Find out if this faith is what you want.

3. Whether you have now found a new faith or have an old one that simply isn't as active as you would like, the next step is to find places to worship, meditate, or otherwise practice your faith. You don't have to systematically try all the churches, synagogues, mosques, and grassy fields in town, for example, but experiment. Unless it truly speaks to you, don't necessarily stop with the first place you go. Faith is an important aspect of the happy and fulfilled life. Don't rush through it.

4. Once you find your place to practice your faith, the next step is to determine your degree of involvement. Would you prefer to mostly practice at home, only going to community events for major festivals or holy days? Would you prefer more frequent contact by attending services once a week? Or maybe you'd prefer to be actively involved by participating in social groups, organizing spiritual practice activities, or frequently attending services?

5. Maintenance is the final step. If you've truly found the right spiritual belief, the right place to practice, and with the right amount of involvement, maintenance won't even require thought. You will feel energized by your involvement. If, on the other hand, you find yourself making excuses to avoid participation, or it begins to feel like work or an obligation, I encourage you to back up to #1 above and start over.

## Mindfulness

There are a handful of self-help books telling people to wake up and stop sleepwalking through life. Mindfulness is exactly that – being fully aware of the present. As a psychologist, I can attest to the fact that too many people are so focused on the past and/or future that the present simply passes them by. Wake up!

Let's go a little deeper into mindfulness.

In the last section on spirituality, I mentioned Buddhism and that's appropriate to remind you of here because mindfulness has its roots in Buddhist meditation. It found its way into the American mainstream several decades ago through the work of Jon Kabat-Zinn who developed the Mindfulness-Based Stress Reduction program (Google that for more about him or his program). Rather than jump into the specific of his program, let's focus on general mindfulness and how you can apply that to your everyday life.

### Practice Exercise – Mindfulness Assessment

If mindfulness is being present in the moment, let's see where you are right now. Ask yourself the following without overly thinking about it:

1. What's going through your mind right now? _____
_____

2. Are you thinking about the present? _____
3. Are you thinking about the past? _____
4. Are you thinking about an event in the future? _____
5. What physical sensations are you aware of? _____
_____
6. What do you hear? _____
7. What do you see? _____
8. What do you smell? _____
9. What do you feel? _____
10. What do you taste? _____

In answering the above questions, how in-the-moment did you start out at and where did you end up? When you think about your day-to-day, are you focused on the present or, like most people, are you thinking about the past or future instead?

When we define mindfulness as a moment-to-moment awareness of the present, we are able to fully inhabit our minds and bodies, aware of all our senses, thoughts, and feelings, without evaluation. Let me repeat that last part – without evaluation.

## How often do you judge yourself (or others)?

Unfortunately, it seems many people are so accustomed to evaluating themselves (whether emotions, thoughts, or actions), that it becomes automatic and interferes with our moment-to-moment satisfaction and happiness. As you learned in *Step 4*, we can unlearn those unhelpful thought processes and learn helpful ones, like the observation without evaluation in mindfulness. This better allows us to live in the moment and actually enjoy each moment!

Our ability to live in the moment is interfered with not just by our internal world but also our external world. How many times have you checked email today? How about Facebook, Twitter, or

Instagram? Can you go an entire meal, movie, or even a workout without some kind of technology (for example, are there televisions at your gym)? Technology is literally all around us and it can be hard to get away. But, if we'd like to increase our mindfulness, one place to start is to put limits on our involvement with technology (and I'll write even more about this in the next section on minimalism).

## Practice Exercise – Increasing Mindfulness

By now you hopefully have a pretty good idea of how present in the moment you are. Let's work on actively increasing that. Starting right now, every hour that you are awake for the next 24 hours (and set an alarm to do this if necessary), I want you to repeat a modified version of the Mindfulness Assessment you did earlier in this section and note the following:

1. What's going through your mind right now? Is it present-, past-, or future-focused? _____
   _____
   _____

2. What physical sensations are you aware of? Try to be aware of all five of your senses. _____
   _____
   _____

Ideally, over your waking hours, you will notice an increase in focus on your present thoughts, feelings, and sensations from the first hour to the last hour.

## Helpful Hint

Repeat the above exercise every few days and see if you begin to notice concrete changes in your degree of mindfulness. Remember, it takes time to unlearn unhelpful habits and learn new healthy habits. Learning to slow down and live in the moment takes time if this is not something to which you are very familiar.

## Minimalism

Minimalism has been defined many different ways – and people have different expectations for what is meant when someone uses the words minimalism or minimalist. What exactly does minimalist mean? I'll start by explaining what it doesn't mean.

Minimalism does not mean you deprive yourself. The intention is not to withhold anything from yourself. In fact, it's quite the opposite. Minimalism is actually taking the time to identify what is important to you and focusing on that. You can see why it's in the chapter on spirituality and mindfulness! And it makes sense that if I focus on what's important to me, then I am in a much better place to also increase my happiness, the purpose of this book.

Minimalism focuses often on physical belongings, so let's start there. If you Google "minimalism", you'll probably find, first and foremost, The Minimalists, Joshua Fields Millburn & Ryan Nicodemus, who I highly recommend you check out. What you will also likely find are lots of websites devoted to decreasing the amount of your physical belongings. Examples include reducing to a capsule wardrobe; paring your items down to only 100, 75, or even 50; living in a tiny house; living car-free; I think you get the point. And all of these can be great, if it helps you focus less on your material possessions and more on the joy and meaning they bring you. Remember that it isn't necessarily about the number of physical items you own, but what they represent.

Beyond physical belongings, minimalism asks us to consider the commitments we make, the activities we engage in, and just generally how we spend our time. If I want to spend more time with my family, but I'm working 80 hours a week, this is not good for my emotional wellbeing. A minimalist considers what activities and people truly bring him or her joy, and focuses on those, learning how to say no and not get pulled into extraneous activities. How many times have you said yes to someone to avoid hurting their feelings or because you were afraid you would miss out on something amazing? As a minimalist, for example, I know who and what are most likely to bring me happiness, and I focus on that (e.g., writing, theater).

As I alluded to last section, technology is a huge time suck in our lives. Now don't get me wrong, I'm a fan of technology. But, you want to be certain that you are benefiting from your use of technology and not that it is metaphorically drowning you. Many, if not all, people have:

- Televisions with DVR, cable, and/or streaming services.
- Smart phones, with instant access to email, social media, and the 24 hour news cycle.
- Inside and outside of the home, constant bombardment of advertisements for the latest and greatest shiny object or service that will guarantee you utter and complete happiness.

Minimalism asks you to consider how much of this actually keeps you connected and happy, and how much of this is a time-suck contributing to a false sense of urgency.

## Practice Exercise – Implementing Minimalism

Based on the areas above, take the three steps below to reduce your overreliance on the excess in your life. This will help you focus on the people and ideas you identified in earlier chapters in the book as able to contribute to your sense of happiness.
- Take an inventory of your physical belongings. An effective method for accomplishing this (I warn you, it will initially take time and likely be emotionally challenging): tackle one room (or

closet, basement, garage) at a time, removing everything from the room, actively considering each item, its value to you (emotionally, not necessarily financially), and whether it brings you joy when you see it and/or touch it. If the answer is yes, return it to the room. If the answer is no, place it in a "sell", "donate", or "trash" pile.

- Take an inventory of your time allocation. Do you spend your time actively engaged in activities that you enjoy? If not, can you create that element? If helpful, chart hour by hour, day by day, where you are spending your time, what you are doing, and with whom. After a week or so, review what you've noted. Armed with this knowledge, begin to eliminate, delegate, or increase activities based on how much joy they bring you. Take your time with this – for example, don't abandon commitments you've already made or quit your job without a plan! Pay attention for how you can make changes going forward.
- Take an inventory of your use of technology. Does the technology you have make your life easier and bring you joy, or has it created more stress? For example, do you DVR bunches of television shows only to experience anxiety about finding time to watch them? Or, do you have 1000 friends on Facebook and spend countless hours scrolling mindlessly through your Newsfeed, while ignoring your significant others in your home? Evaluate everything and begin to eliminate where necessary. For example, in our home, we cut cable and we keep phones off during dinner.

## Helpful Hint

If the above practice exercise has you hyperventilating with the idea of cutting back on any or all of the physical belongings, commitments, and technology time wasters, that's okay. The Internet is awash in examples for how to approach each of the above in different ways. If what I've written doesn't work exactly for you, don't give up. Do some online research and find other options.

Remember, minimalism will not look the same for everybody. Some people love that they can get down to only 40 articles of clothing. Some love that they don't have a television in their homes. Some simply love the freedom to choose not to engage with any of this stuff that doesn't bring them happiness. Do what works for you in your situation. The goal is to own belongings that bring you joy, make commitments that bring you joy, and use technology to bring you joy. Do you see the theme? Most people find that by focusing on what truly brings them joy, they begin to want less "stuff" or "noise" in their life that interferes with that true joy.

## Gratitude

Gratitude means to be thankful for something that you have or that someone has done for you. There are lots of fancier definitions and ways to parse that out, but at its core, this is what it means to be grateful. Gratitude impacts happiness by helping us appreciate what we have, appreciate what others do for us, and strengthen relationships through our expression of that gratitude to others.

### How easy or not is it for you to say thank you?

Sometimes people struggle to express gratitude for a fairly simple reason; we believe the person "should" have done whatever it is that they did, therefore no thanks are needed. For example, if you believe that people "should" hold the door open for other people, then when somebody does it for you, you may not feel the need to say thank you.

Sometimes people struggle to express gratitude because they believe the person already knows how they feel and they genuinely don't believe it necessary to say out loud. For example, if you believe your spouse knows you appreciate that s/he does most of the cooking, you may not feel it necessary to actually say thank you for doing the cooking.

The problem with both of the above situations is that, when someone chooses to do something nice for us, that is a choice. Regardless of whether something is socially expected or happens often, the person engaging in the activity has chosen to do that nice thing and expressing gratitude is our way of acknowledging that choice. And when we acknowledge that choice to do something nice, we feel good, they feel good, and we're both more likely to go out and make more positive choices.

What about experiences that do not involve other people? Are you able to recognize and appreciate all of the good things that happen to you every day? Or do you focus on the negative? Let's do a little mini-experiment:

## Practice Exercise – Going to the Movies

"Monday afternoon I had plans to see a movie with a friend. When I went out to my car, it wouldn't start. My neighbor gave me a jump and I was only about ten minutes late leaving. Traffic was light, though, so I reached my friend's house pretty quickly. We arrived at the movie theater as it began to rain; we circled a bit before finding a spot near the back. Luckily, there was no line when we bought our tickets, so we got in immediately. There was a line at the snack bar, but they were having a 2-for-1 sale. The theater wasn't too crowded, so we got to sit where we wanted. Our movie was a quieter drama and periodically we heard the booms of the action movie next door. After the movie, the rain had stopped and I took my friend home."

- Now, close your eyes for a moment and retell that story as if it happened to you. What were the highlights of the story?

- For many people struggling with happiness, they find that in retelling this story, they focus on the negative – the car wouldn't start, it was raining, they could hear the movie next door. They overlook the positive – light traffic, no line for tickets, 2-for-1 sale on snacks. If that was you, take that knowledge and begin to make changes.

Gratitude is about appreciating the things that people do for us AND the good things that simply happen, big and small. Many people either overly focus on the negative throughout their day or only focus on the big positives, like a great vacation. Your goal is to notice and appreciate lots of things throughout the day that maybe right now you overlook. For example, I can enjoy getting a good parking spot or my awesome café mocha in the morning.

## Practice Exercise – Gratitude Journal

If recognizing the good things that you experience everyday is something you struggle with, you can learn to strengthen that muscle through use of a Gratitude Journal.

- Before bed every night, take the time to write down at least three things that you were grateful for that day.
- Keep this journal for at least a couple of weeks – in my therapy group, the participants keep this journal for ten weeks.

These can be big, like a promotion at work, or they can be small, like a sunny day. They also can involve other people, like someone buying your lunch, or they can be solo, like completing your workout for the day. The goal is for the recognition of these positive things, and expression of thanks if another person was involved, to become your new automatic habit.

## Vignette

Katriona described her concern as a lack of spiritual fulfillment. She felt there was something missing from an otherwise satisfying life. Upon questioning, I learned that she had moved to town just under a year prior and had become quite active at work and in the community. The only thing different from her life before was spiritual involvement. Katriona had attended church every week, sometimes twice a week, sang in the church choir, and helped out at church functions on a regular basis. Since she had been to town she had been reluctant to find a new church.

When asked to reflect on the reasons she was reluctant to find a new church, Katriona identified two primary concerns. Her first concern was that no church she could find would stand up to her wonderful memories of her former church. Her second concern was that she would not be as accepted in a new church in a new town, that she would forever be an outsider.

Addressing Katriona's second concern first, I asked her if she had been born in her previous town. She responded no. I then asked how old she had been when she joined her previous church. Twenty-five was the answer. Did she feel like an outsider when she joined that prior church? Katriona immediately got my meaning and reflected on the fact that she was quickly accepted into her previous church and that she never really felt like an outsider.

Katriona's broader fears were addressed second, that any new church would never be as wonderful as her former. I asked Katriona questions about the church she attended before the most recent one. She had been a member of that congregation for only a couple of years. She was not as entrenched in the activities of that church as she was in the later church. Katriona realized that although perhaps a new church would not immediately live up to her old standards, she was quite likely to create new memories and build strong connections the longer she remained involved.

Katriona's first homework assignment then was to identify all the churches in town in her religious preference. After obtaining that list, she was to query individuals she knew to ascertain if any of them attended any of those churches. If so, she was to get their opinions. If not, she could explore the options of trying an unknown church within her religious preference or trying one outside of her specific faith if a friend seemed particularly enamored of his or her church.

Through this method, Katriona developed a list of three local churches. Her next assignment was to attend church services at least twice at each. This would allow her to speak with other members about what they liked and didn't like about their churches. It would also give her a chance to determine how active the church was in other areas, such as social events, volunteering opportunities, and availability of additional church involvement, like the choir.

By attending each church twice, Katriona not only learned a great deal about the churches and their members, she ended up feeling a connection to one in particular and found her new spiritual home. She became ensconced in everything the church had to offer and quickly filled that hole in her spiritual life.

## Chapter Purpose

The purpose of this chapter was to assist you in determining whether or not you are satisfied spiritually; whether or not you are satisfied with your physical belongings and time commitments; and whether or not you are able to live in the moment, appreciating what you have and what others do for you. Over the course of the chapter, you were asked to consider what physically, emotionally, and spiritually takes up time and space in your life, whether or not this is satisfactory, and what you could do to begin to make changes.

## Practice Exercise Checklist

- Spiritual Identification – Belief in something bigger than the self is innately connected to happiness. This practice exercise asks you to consider your spiritual satisfaction and offers steps to make changes if appropriate.

- Mindfulness Assessment – Consider how in-the-moment you are by answering a series of basic questions just where you are, reading this chapter. Many people find themselves thinking about the past or the future instead of simply enjoying today's moments.

- Increasing Mindfulness – Once you've identified your basic level of mindfulness, repeat a modified version of the Mindfulness Assessment once an hour for all the hours you're awake in a 24 hour period. Note the thoughts going through your mind and the physical sensations, repeating the assessment as needed to increase your ability to stay focused in a given moment.

- Implementing Minimalism – Consider what you have in your life and whether it contributes to your happiness. There are three steps to assess and reduce physical belongings, time commitments, and technology overload, as appropriate to your individual lifestyle.

- Going to the Movies – What we choose to focus on has such an impact on emotion, this practice exercise asks you to read a story and then retell it in your own words, noting whether you mostly focused on the positive events in the story or the negative.

- Gratitude Journal – The final practice exercise of the chapter asks you to write down at least three things big or small that you were grateful for during the day. By keeping the journal for **at least** a couple of weeks (longer if possible) you'll find the recognition of these positive things, and expression of thanks if another person was involved, becomes your new automatic habit.

With the bulk of our information on how to attain happiness presented, it's time to move on to the final chapter – *Trust*. No matter what else you do, almost all people need to share their lives with others. And that takes trust. It's important enough, and sometimes elusive enough, to warrant its very own chapter.

# STEP 9
# TRUST

*The best way to find out if you can trust somebody is to trust them.*
Ernest Hemingway (Writer)

Defining trust is fairly easy. The repeated definition I found online for the word is, to rely on the integrity, ability, or character of a person or thing. Let's take apart that definition. To rely means to depend on. Integrity is everything from honesty to personal values. Ability is the means to accomplish what you intend. Character may be the moral features of a being. So, to trust is to depend on a being's ability to be honest to their moral and personal values. Not always considered is that trust is that act of placing confidence in both yourself and another.

*Why is trust important?*

We all have an intuitive sense of why trust is important in our lives, but I bet most of us have never stopped to think about exactly why trust is not just important, but absolutely critical to our functioning as individuals, as well as within society.

We as human animals could not live without trust. Human society requires a certain level of trust among people just to survive, let alone thrive. I trust that food will appear in the supermarket that is reasonably fresh. I trust that when I drive my car the other drivers will follow the same rules of the road (maybe that's not the best example!) On a more primitive level, I trust that my neighbor will not murder me. I trust that I can walk down the street without being attacked. Watching the news, we know that people break this social contract every day. This is why we feel so violated.

But, we're looking for authentic happiness – to thrive, not just survive. What role does trust play in happiness for individuals and within society? Trust is crucial to establishing connections and relationships. When we know we can trust someone, there is a comfort and confidence that allows us to do what we need, secure in the knowledge that the other is trustworthy. We are able to assess our interactions with others, their histories with us, to know whether or not trust is appropriately placed. Happiness is practically impossible without the comfort of knowing we have trust.

## Trust means to believe.

In yourself. In others. In society as a whole. We falter when we do not have that trust in all three. Trust is at the core of every single successful relationship – to ourselves, in romantic endeavors, in business alliances, with family members, with every single member of society. It is at the heart of the social contract, which is a political term that emphasizes stability in society.

## Practice Exercise – Trusting Yourself

Answer the following questions, being as honest as possible, even if the answers make you uncomfortable:
1. Do you trust yourself? _____
2. Do you believe yourself to be trustworthy? _____
3. When you honestly consider your internal thoughts and your external behavior, how do you measure up? _____

I ask those questions to encourage you to accurately assess your own degree of trust in yourself. If you are unable to trust yourself, either because you do not believe yourself to be trustworthy or actually are not trustworthy, then you must work on that before working to build trust with others. And I'm here to help! Just remember that trust truly is a two-way street.

*How do you build trust?*

It is not always so easy just to say, "be more trusting and be more trustworthy". Sometimes we need a little guidance and specific recommendations. This next section will provide seven ways to build trust in yourself and nine ways to build trust with others. The purpose is to give you that extra boost along the trust continuum.

For this first part of seven ways to build or increase trust in yourself, it's important to focus on the little things that are meaningful in and of themselves but that also combine to be extraordinary. Many of these will also apply to building trust with others, but right now I want your focus to be inward.

1. Demonstrate dependability by doing what you say you will. Have your word mean something to yourself, such that if you make a commitment, you follow through. I'm specifically talking here about committing to yourself, by the way, not to others. The corollary to that admonition is a reminder to avoid taking on too much, or taking on something you don't really want to do.

Helpful Hint – Be aware of your self-promises. If you say "I'm going to exercise four days this week", then do it. If you say you're going to read two chapters for sociology class, then do it. The key is to develop belief in your own word, that if you tell yourself you will engage in a particular activity, that you have no doubt that you will.

2. Speak honestly to yourself by not denying, making excuses, or blaming others to make yourself look or feel better. Those thoughts may or may not work in the short term but definitely don't in the long term. Over time, you will find it increasingly difficult to identify where the lies and misinformation end and the truth or reality begins.

Helpful Hint – Accept your strengths and weaknesses with grace and honesty. For example, if you fail to get promoted over a colleague, don't badmouth the colleague or the company, saying there was some other reason for the promotion, just to make yourself feel better. Accept it and begin preparing for the next opportunity.

3. Respect your own opinions, beliefs, and attitudes, whether others are in agreement or not (though be careful not to be closed off to new information that may alter your opinions). In essence, I'm asking you to believe in yourself, in your worth as a person. Trust that you are deserving of respect.

Helpful Hint – Everyone experiences self-doubt, but it's important not to let it become your way of being. If you disagree with someone over a hotly contested topic, don't immediately defer to the other person, believing that your opinion is somehow less valuable. Remain open to legitimate new information while respecting your own values.

4. Acknowledge doubts by recognizing that nobody knows everything, including you, nor are they expected to. No matter how much we think we know, there's always more to learn and that's perfectly okay. Neither can we predict the future. At best, we can make educated guesses.

Helpful Hint – Stop trying to predict the future and assume you know an outcome before it occurs. For example, if you want to apply for a new job, but are concerned you won't be hired, acknowledge that uncertainty and move forward with the application. Trust in your ability to do your best regardless of outcome.

5. Admit to and learn from mistakes, as doing so is the natural follow-up to acknowledging doubts. Nobody is perfect. Perfection is impossible to attain. Yet, people truly struggle with this one. That's where some perfectionist tendencies come from. Admitting mistakes is tantamount to failure and weakness for so many, but the opposite is true. It takes genuine strength to admit when we've been wrong. Even better, use your mistakes as learning experiences so you may trust in yourself to avoid making the same mistake in the future.

Helpful Hint – Acknowledge to yourself when you've goofed. For example, say you realize at work that you completed the wrong form for a project. You could pretend that you didn't and hope nobody can tie you to it; you could blame someone else for not better explaining what you needed to do; or you can be honest and admit that you completed the wrong form. By determining where you went wrong, you will be able to ensure success the next time without dwelling on the mistake.

6. Forgiving yourself is the obvious next step from admitting mistakes. Recognize that you need to let go of what you may have done wrong. If you need to make amends, depending on the severity of the mistake, then certainly do so, but holding on to regret helps no one. Minimize your regret for having made the mistake, since everyone makes them, by learning and moving on.

Helpful Hint – Apologize as necessary and give yourself permission to forgive yourself. For example, if you slept through your alarm clock and left a friend hanging, of course you're going to feel horrible. It was not intentional, but it occurred. Acknowledge it by apologizing to your friend. Learn to set multiple alarms when it's really important or you have a concern about waking up. Let go of your regret; minimize your chances of doing it again in the future.

7. Explore by moving outside of your comfort zone. People sometimes find themselves in a rut for a variety of reasons, one of

which could be lack of trust in themselves or a fear of failure that new adventures will be successful. Try something new without any expectations and celebrate the trying.

Helpful Hint – Do something either completely new or different, or something you've always wanted to but were afraid to try. For example, if you've always wanted to try trapeze, do it. Once you've done it, you can share pictures and videos of the attempt and/or accomplishment for friends and family to celebrate with you (and maybe even inspire one of them to try).

## Building Trust in Others

Once you begin to trust yourself, it is time to look to your relationships. Consider both your close personal ones and impersonal stranger ones (because yes, we have relationships with everyone with whom we interact). Trust in relationships is critical for the functioning of society. Therefore, moving forward from the past section, I will present nine ways to build trust in your relationships with others. Some are quite similar to ways to build trust in yourself, but the focus now is outward.

The first three ways to build trust in a relationship are related to acting with integrity by demonstrating honesty, loyalty, and fairness to others.

1. Demonstrate trustworthiness with the small stuff. People don't need big sweeping gestures to know whether or not they can trust you. In fact, other people typically will want to believe they can trust you in the little things before they will even consider trusting you with the big things. This is logical. I'm not going to trust you to organize a party if you can't even be on time for the first organizational meeting.

Helpful Hint – Keep your word. It's as simple as that. If you make a promise, you keep it. You will build trust when people know they can count on you. The corollary to this is to always tell the truth. Your word must be honest. All it takes is one lie for people to lose complete trust in you on every level.

2. Remain loyal by maintaining the confidences of others. In other words, don't be a gossip. Don't tell the juicy information that you are privy to in order to demonstrate how in-the-know you are or to provide others with salacious material. When someone opens up and tells you something that may be difficult for them in some way, whether because it was painful, shameful, or embarrassing, it is not your story to tell. Let me repeat that, it is not your story to tell.

Helpful Hint – What a person tells you in a relationship needs to stay in that relationship. Think about how you would feel if you confided in someone, only to have someone else later comment on it.
- Would you feel betrayed? Of course you would.
- Would you trust that same confidante again? Of course you wouldn't.

Don't be that untrustworthy person. The easiest way to accomplish this is don't talk about a person who isn't physically present.

3. Treat people fairly by applying the Golden Rule: Do unto others as you would have them do unto you. It's pretty straightforward, even if not always so easy to practice.

Helpful Hint – Consider the following explicitly:
- Do not treat people preferentially.
- Do not stereotype.
- Do not be disingenuous.

Instead:
- Be magnanimous.
- Treat all equally.
- Do for others without expectation of some kind of reward in return (this last seems to be one that people struggle with).

## Practice Exercise – Perspective Taking

There is one simple technique for increasing trust in almost any situation: Before you say or do anything, try taking the other person's perspective. I want you to practice that by watching for an opportunity in the next week where you notice you are upset with someone else and want to say something to that person:

1. Consider first why they might have said or did what they did. Imagine you are them.
2. How do you imagine they would feel about your intended reaction (comment or action)?
3. Try also imagining you are the one the words are being spoken about or the action is concerning. Would you like it or dislike it?

This may take some effort at first, but the rewards are innumerable as people learn you are empathetic and kind. It's similar to the expression, "walk a mile in another's shoes". You may not be able to do exactly that, but you can imagine it, can't you? Take the other person's perspective.

The next three ways to build trust can be applied toward building a positive reputation. It takes time and effort to build a good reputation, but this immeasurably increases others' trust in you. These next three are doing a good job, exceeding the expectations of others, and simply doing things for others.

4. Doing a job well is one of the best ways to build a reputation such that people will trust you to remain competent in the future. That's completely logical, right? Your work represents who you are (whether it's paid, volunteer, or simply for fun). Always strive to do the best that you can. By continuing to try your best, no matter how

tough it becomes, you demonstrate to everyone who witnesses that you are someone who will possibly work that hard for them if the occasion arose.

Helpful Hint – Related to what's written above, try to only engage in activities that you really like. Your motivation will remain at its peak for the most part because you will have wanted to do what you're doing. The reality is that most people engage in activities they feel lukewarm about some of the time; suck it up and still try your best. Your work is a reflection of you whether you want to do it or not. What will build more trust for you: smiling and doing your absolute best, or grumbling and whining about how you don't want to be there? Exactly.

5. Exceeding or (at least) satisfying expectations is the end result of persevering to do a job well. When people see or hear about how you are reliable and dependable, that you can be counted on when the chips are down, they will begin to expect that from you. This is a good thing! If you continue to satisfy or exceed those expectations, you will continue to build that trust.

Helpful Hint – Determine the expectations of others and do your best to satisfy or exceed them every single time. If you start to falter, remember the fragility of the trust you are building and how important your actions are in the situation. The greater the effort, the higher the trust. To use visual aids, you can either have a bank account growing with regular deposits, or write bouncing checks all over town. Which would you prefer?

6. Choosing options that are in the best interests of others will allow you to demonstrate to them that you care about and for them. You don't want to go too far in this direction, becoming a doormat who puts everyone's needs above your own. Just remember that choosing to say and do things that benefit the other person will certainly increase that individual's trust in you.

Helpful Hint: Consider that doing things for other people will result in good feelings within yourself, good feelings in the other person, and, possibly, the person doing something for you later.

The final three ways of increasing trust in relationships involve admitting mistakes, only asking of others what we would do, and sharing personal information while spending time with the people important to us.

7. Apologizing when you make a mistake is an amazingly effective way of building trust in a relationship. This is for two reasons. One, as mentioned earlier, people seem to really struggle with admitting mistakes so the person will likely be impressed that you have openly done so. Two, taking responsibility for your choices will help alleviate at least some of the harm done by the bad choice.

Helpful Hint – Be aware of opportunities to apologize when you make a mistake. That may sound odd; how can you miss when you've messed up? Usually we're acutely aware of transgressions. The key here is to watch for the opportunities to actually make the apology after the fact. They may not be as obvious as you think, causing you to miss opportune moments.

8. Never asking others to do anything you would not do yourself is related to perspective taking. Before ever asking for a favor in your personal life or delegating a job in the office, consider whether or not you would be willing to do the job yourself.

Helpful Hint – It's never a bad idea to consider another person's perspective. In this scenario, it's important to be certain you are not taking advantage. For example, if you are coordinating a fundraising dinner, think before you ask someone to cold call potential donors.

9. Spending time with another person and sharing information about yourself are excellent ways to build trust in a relationship. In

our ever-shrinking world, it can be easy to spend less and less time with people in the physical world. And with the opportunities to post incessant life updates online about our day-to-day minutia, we seem to be pretty good about sharing personal information. However…

## Are you simply providing the equivalent of sound bites to surface friends?

Helpful Hint – As someone who is on LinkedIn, Twitter, Instagram, and Facebook myself, for example, it can become very easy to be swept up in the idea that you are maintaining contact with your friends adequately and sharing real information. Just because you know that someone's training for a marathon because it was a Facebook status, however, does not mean you're really staying in touch. Consider also the quality of the information you are sharing. Do you take the time to think about how you are feeling and have an actual discussion with a friend? Demonstrating that you want real-time contact and trust them enough to share personal information will naturally engender reciprocal trust.

### Practice Exercises to Identify Your Levels of Trust

Having provided specific guidance on everyday ways to enhance your trust in yourself and others, I want to take what may likely seem to be a step backward. I want you to directly explore your personal levels of trust in yourself and in others. The reason I provided the guidance above first is because I wanted to prime you to begin thinking about what activities and thoughts you may or may not already engage in, with regard to being trusting and trustworthy. Now, it's time to look inward.

These first three practice exercises are intended to get you thinking about how much trust you have in yourself, as well as how easily (or not) you trust other people. Sometimes we have certain ideas about our strengths and weaknesses that may not be entirely accurate, and these practice exercise are intended to expose your internal workings a bit, to identify where you fall on the continuum between completely trusting and trustworthy to completely untrusting and untrustworthy.

## Practice Exercise – Indicators of Trust

Track your interactions with people for a full week. You can use any of the tracking methods you've used in the program so far. Try to do this practice exercise as much in the moment as you can, before the information from the interaction fades or becomes distorted. For each situation, especially ones with emotional resonance, immediately note any changes you experience during the encounter:

- Are you finding that you feel tension anywhere in your body?
- Do you feel queasy or physically ill?
- How would you describe your emotional reaction to the conversation?
- Do you feel anxious, frustrated, or uncertain?

If you answered "yes" to many or most of those questions, that suggests distrust for the other person. If you answered "no" to most of those questions, that suggests trust (or neutrality) of the other person. At the end of the week, review your entries in the notebook.

- Do you have more entries suggesting trust or distrust?
- Does the ratio surprise you?

The more entries suggesting distrust that you have, the more likely it is that you have difficulty trusting others.

## Helpful Hint

If you find that you have a hard time reading your body signals, be more explicit. Ask yourself directly if you trust the other person – if you have children or beloved companion animals, ask yourself, "Would I let this person be responsible for them?" Pay attention to your immediate response, as it is likely the authentic one.

## Practice Exercise – Thoughts Related to Trust

Answer the following questions with the first response that comes to mind, without over-analyzing. There are no right or wrong answers. I'm looking for gut responses.

*Answer true or false to the following:*
- _____1. Most people can be trusted.
- _____2. It's easy to trust close family and friends.
- _____3. My parent(s) or guardian was always there for me.
- _____4. My friends and family are there for me.
- _____5. Communication was clear in my family growing up.
- _____6. I know that people will help me if I need it.
- _____7. Telling the truth was important growing up.
- _____8. I believe my friends and family throughout my life have told the truth.
- _____9. I have lots of friends and family and/or I'm in a happy, committed relationship.

The more "true" answers you honestly gave, the more trusting you likely are. The more "false" answers you gave, the less trusting you likely are. This might seem like, "well, duh", but this exercise helps to highlight your perceptions of your personal world and the people who populate it. If your instinctual answers to the above questions suggest this is an area in need of development, pay attention to that.

## Practice Exercise – Trusting to Connect

Your ability to connect with others is an excellent gauge of how trusting you are. If you do not trust the people with whom you interact, you will struggle to connect with them. On the flip side, it may also mean that people do not trust you, so keep that in mind, as well. Using a 7-point scale, rate each of your most important relationships (family, friends, and colleagues) on a scale of 1 to 7, where 1 = emotionally removed, 4 = perfectly connected, and 7 = overly trusting to the point of being at risk for hurt.

1. _____
2. _____
3. _____
4. _____
5. _____
6. _____
7. _____

What do you notice? Are there consistently more lower or higher numbers? Does it evenly vary between types of relationships? Do the numbers seem completely random? Remember, there are no right or wrong answers. When you review your responses, what does your instinct tell you about them? Are you connected and thus trusting and trusted, or maybe less than you would like?

## Exercises to Enhance Your Trust in Yourself and in Others

Now that you have a better idea of your level of trust in yourself and your trust in others, whether close friends, family, acquaintances, or strangers, try the below exercises to increase all of those levels. Even if you didn't identify from the above exercises that you have "trust issues" so to speak, it never hurts to develop improved trust.

## Practice Exercise – Improving Trust in Yourself

Do you struggle to decide between options? When you make a choice, do you incessantly weigh the pros and cons beforehand and then still second guess the route you chose? Do you ignore "gut feelings" then experience self-doubt about how you were feeling?

The next time you have a choice to make, I want you to use one of the following. If choosing between two options and you've done all your research, but you're not sure what to do, I want you to take out a quarter, assign each option to heads or tails, and flip the coin. Really. I want you to flip a coin. Ah, but here's the catch. When the quarter lands and you know what your random outcome is, I want you to immediately note how you feel. Happy or disappointed?

- If you were happy at the coin flip, pick that random response.
- If you were disappointed, then pick the option assigned to the side of the quarter that's underneath.

Over time, I want you to begin leaning in one direction or another before flipping the coin, so that you can note how often your leaning is the way you end up going. With practice, you will find that you're initially choosing the eventual outcome, thus increasing your trust in your gut instincts.

If your options number more than two, you can do this same exercise by labeling strips of paper with the options, placing them in a hat, or other non-transparent receptacle, and otherwise following the same instructions when you draw out varying slips. It'll be a little more complicated because you may have to repeat the exercise if each paper elicits a sense of disappointment (because you won't know which of the remaining options in the hat is the one you really want). But, it will still work.

## Helpful Hint

You may find it helpful to start either of the above with minor choices like where to go to dinner, believe it or not. Learning to trust your instincts with less life changing options can help you to improve your trust in yourself before facing larger more important choices.

## Practice Exercise – Forgiving to Build Trust

Consider at least three people who hurt you in some way. They can be family or friends. The hurt could have occurred yesterday or thirty years ago. If it springs to mind, it's obviously important to you. Once you have the three people and the way they've hurt you in mind, I want you to take a radical leap. Take their perspective on what has happened. Consider possible motives for the behavior, consider alternate explanations for their choices, and finally, specifically consider positive motives. It doesn't matter if you ever know the real motivation, but consider whether the hurt could have been accidental, or the result of a misunderstanding. As you take the other people's perspectives, note how that changes your emotions and your thoughts of the person and the incident. Begin to practice the idea of assumed benevolence, that people as a default will do the right thing.

## Helpful Hint

If your situations involved serious harm, such as assault or molestation, this exercise will likely be a lot harder. It's better to select more everyday kinds of hurt, at least initially.

## Practice Exercise – Modifying Thoughts to Improve Trust

Track your interactions with people **again** for another week. However, this time I want you to work to change your internal reactions to people and your thoughts about the interactions, keeping the following in mind:

- Neither you nor the other person has all the answers.
- Neither you nor the other person could have all the information necessary in every instance to make the perfect choice in every situation.
- Recognize that communication is also imperfect and that misunderstandings occur.

With these thoughts in mind, note how you interpret your interactions and how your mind and body respond differently over time. The idea is that by repeating the initial practice exercise you will notice that you have fewer of the physical and emotional responses suggestive of distrust. Did it work? I truly hope so.

## Vignette

Charlie walked into my office, sat down, and said very little of substance over the next 45 minutes. Oh, sure, he talked about this and that, and easily filled the time with speech. When the appointment ended, I knew that there was a deeper issue than what he ostensibly came to the appointment for. I asked him to do an exercise for me between that appointment and his first follow-up visit. He was surprised, but agreed to do so.

What I asked Charlie to do was to track his interactions with people for two weeks. I instructed him to buy a notebook and carry it with him everywhere that he went. I encouraged him to write down what I asked as much in the moment as possible, for the very reasons

I gave earlier: The greater the amount of time that passes, the more inaccurate your memories become.

For the first week, with each encounter with someone, especially any of importance, I asked him to immediately note any physical changes he experienced during the encounter. Did he notice physical tension? Did he notice any queasiness? What was his emotional reaction to the encounter? Did he have a negative emotion, whether anxiety, frustration, or uncertainty?

After reviewing his responses for the first week, he was surprised to notice how many of his responses suggested distrust of others. We spent time processing this new knowledge and discussing the nature of trust before I gave him the assignment for the second week. I asked him to track his interactions with people again, but added the step of working to change his internal reactions to people and his thoughts about the interactions, by considering that neither he nor the other person in each encounter has all the answers, is capable of having perfect information, and could be misunderstood. He engaged in this exercise across several appointments until finally, when he returned for one appointment, he was all smiles. He explained that he noticed that his physical and emotional responses had finally altered almost completely. He knew this was due to increased trust in others, based on his own thoughts about people and how he felt more relaxed around them.

## Chapter Purpose

Trust is not typically either-or; in other words, you likely have varying degrees of trust both in yourself and toward other people around you. The purpose of this chapter was to assist you in assessing your degrees of trust in yourself and others. Given my premise that trust underlies nearly every relationship and interaction, the chapter offered lots of practical guidance and recommendations to begin increasing your trust in yourself and others.

## Practice Exercise Checklist

- Trusting Yourself – Three not-so-simple questions begin the first practice exercise, designed to encourage you to accurately assess your own degree of trust in yourself. If you are unable to trust yourself, either because you do not believe yourself to be trustworthy or actually are not trustworthy, then you must work on that before working to build trust with others.

- Perspective Taking – The second practice exercise begins with the premise that perspective taking is one basic technique for increasing trust in almost any situation. Recognizing this may be challenging, trying to understand where another is coming from will result in increased goodwill for yourself and for others.

- Indicators of Trust – One way to assess your level of trust in others is to track your interactions with people for a week and note any physical or emotional changes, particularly unpleasant changes, occurring during the encounter. The more you experience discomfort, the more it suggests distrust of the people with whom you are interacting.

- Thoughts Related to Trust – Although asked only to answer nine true-or-false statements without overanalyzing your responses, your answers highlight your perceptions of your personal world and the people who populate it. If your instinctual answers to the questions suggest this is an area in need of development, pay attention to that.

- Trusting to Connect – This practice exercise gauges how trusting you are (as well as how trustworthy others may view you). You are asked to rate each of your most important relationships on how connected you feel to them. Your answers shine a light on how connected and thus trusting and trusted you are.

- Improving Trust in Yourself – Flip a coin when you're struggling to make a decision between two options. The catch is that you evaluate and make your choice based on how you feel once you know your random outcome. The goal is that over time you will increase your trust in your gut instincts.

- Forgiving to Build Trust – Being able to forgive is intimately connected to increasing trust in yourself and others. Actively taking the perspective of three people who have wronged you, you can begin to practice the idea of assumed benevolence.

- Modifying Thoughts to Improve Trust – The final practice exercise of the chapter asks you to again track your interactions with people for another week. This time, you are asked to actively work on modifying the way you're thinking about and interpreting the situations, such that over time you will notice fewer physical and emotional indicators of distrust.

*Remember: It takes years to build up trust, and only seconds to destroy it.*
Anonymous

Have you noticed improvement from the beginning of the chapter? If not, I'd like you to seriously consider the possibility that more structured and involved individual therapy may be warranted to address any underlying significant blocks to trust. And don't worry. All it means is that you may need a little focused guidance to help you get back on the path.

## Congratulations!

You have just completed the final step in the *9 Steps to Authentic Happiness*! If you have truly absorbed and practiced the information and recommendations contained herein, you are that much further along the path to true, authentic happiness. There's just one final piece to present…please continue on to the final chapter.

DR. HEATHER SILVIO

# FINAL THOUGHTS

As promised in the *Introduction*, there was nothing new in this book. I don't say that to downplay my addition to the self-help oeuvre. I say that because truly, for the most part, there isn't anything new under the sun. My goal was to bring together enough of the information spread far and wide into a single, directed, specific recommendation-filled plan to map out the way to achieving authentic happiness. It really isn't complicated – not to say that it's easy either, of course. And, if you actually complete the self-exploration exercises and implement the recommendations provided, you can make the necessary changes to create authentic happiness.

*Perfection is unattainable and its pursuit inevitably leads to disappointment*

Having written the above paragraph, let me now slightly contradict myself! **Life is a journey, not a destination.** Maybe too pithy for some, but truly revelatory if you internalize the words. Use these nine steps as guidance while you move through the world, recognizing that Happiness is not a capital-letter end state, but rather that there is always something new you can learn, experience, or do. If you aren't learning and growing, then you're dead. I truly believe that far too many people sleepwalk through life, simply accepting their circumstances without ever even searching for, let alone finding, their bliss.

Remember the old adage about telling people new things:

Tell 'em what you're going to tell 'em. Tell 'em what you have to tell 'em. And then tell 'em what you told 'em.

That's the purpose of this concluding chapter. I'm going to present a paragraph summary of each *Step* and list out the *Step's* practice exercises. I'm doing this to highlight how far you've come and what you've learned. Sometimes when we reach the ending, we've forgotten the beginning! I hope to help the information stick.

## **Part 1 Body**: Step 1 Diet

Physical health is essential to overall wellbeing and happiness. In this chapter, I discussed the roles of balanced eating, emotional eating, alcohol consumption, and hydration on health. There were several practice exercises intended to help you self-assess and implement changes.

### Practice Exercise Checklist

- Food Diary – If you want to effectively evaluate your eating patterns, you start with a basic log of every time you eat or drink anything for two weeks.

- Nutrient Needs – Once you have your Food Diary, you evaluate it to determine if your nutrient needs are being met for optimal functioning by reviewing whether or not each day's meals and snacks include a protein, grain, and fruit/vegetable.

- Planning Your Meals – Identifying recipes through cookbooks or online sources, you can then plan your week's meals/snacks, grocery shop with the list of needed ingredients, and experiment with at least one new recipe each week.

- Dietary Lifestyle – Determining whether or not what you're eating reflects who you are and what you want to accomplish with your diet may necessitate moving in the direction of a more specific dietary lifestyle choice, such as becoming a vegetarian or going gluten-free.

- (Optional) Elimination Diet – Many people have allergies or food sensitivities. If you've noticed you simply don't feel well, try a simple elimination diet of cutting out one food item for 2-4 weeks, or a more complex elimination diet of cutting out gluten, dairy, sugar, and alcohol for 2-4 weeks, and based on how you feel, you can either stop there, or add items back in one at a time to see where the sensitivities may be.

- Uncovering Emotional Eating – Repeat the Food Diary exercise for two weeks, additionally noting thoughts and feelings when eating or drinking, including whether or not you are actually hungry, and then making the recommended immediate, short, and long term changes noted in the chapter.

- Alcohol Consumption (if you drink at all) – Track your alcohol consumption for two weeks, specifically noting where you are drinking; what your feelings are before, during, and after you drink; and how you feel physically immediately after consumption and the next day. Did your alcohol consumption result in positive or negative emotional and physical feelings?

- Water Consumption – Determine whether you are staying adequately hydrated by reviewing the liquid consumption noted in your Food and Alcohol Diaries, and whether you felt any of the symptoms of dehydration. If so, you can follow up with the Helpful Hints described.

## Step 2 Physical Activity

Next the focus shifted to how physical activity is critical for optimal health in body, mind, and spirit. In this chapter, I discussed healthy weight, levels and types of exercise, and the importance of motivation in making physical lifestyle changes.

## Practice Exercise Checklist

- Determining Healthy Weight – One of the best places to start is with determining whether or not you are at a healthy body weight; this practice exercise offers the height/weight chart, calculating BMI, and skinfold thickness measurement as options.

- Fitness Goals – By writing down what your fitness goals are, which may be quite general at this stage, it helps to clarify your hopes and desires moving forward.

- Exercise Log – If you want to effectively determine and evaluate your exercise patterns, start with a basic log of every time you exercise for two weeks, noting activity (cardio, strength, and/or flexibility), length of time, and intensity.

- Hurdling Excuses – It can become quite easy to rationalize skipping a workout; the first step in overcoming excuses is to identify them, which this practice exercise encourages you to do, before offering solutions.

- Identifying Specific Goals – "Lose weight" may be a common goal, but it is also too general. Staying focused and motivated is easier with more specific goals, e.g., lose one pound per week.

- Identifying Rewards – Maintaining motivation can be helped by rewarding ourselves for meeting short- and long-term exercise goals, especially if we can tie the reward into physical activity, e.g., new workout gear for attending six months of yoga classes.

- Non-Exercise Physical Activity – Exercise is a dirty word for some people so it's important to identify the physical activity we do on a daily basis, whether through housework, yard work, grocery shopping, walking through parking lots, etc.

## Step 3 Sleep & Meditation

As the final chapter under the *Body* heading, I covered sleep and meditation for rejuvenation; this was somewhat of a bridge step to *Part 2 Mind*. By the end of the chapter, you better understood your own sleep patterns and had the opportunity to practice meditation.

## Practice Exercise Checklist

- Sleep Diary – Before you can possibly make any adjustments to your sleep, you have to determine how much you're really getting. People are notoriously bad at guesstimating this, which is why I recommend keeping a sleep diary for two weeks, where you note when you believe you fell asleep, when you woke up, if you had additional night wakings, or if you took naps during the day. Finally, note how you felt after each night's rest, so you can begin to see how you're truly doing.

- Deep Breathing – As a relaxation exercise, deep breathing can also work wonders for sleep. This version of relaxation breathing asks you to do a minimum of 10 breaths, breathing in through the nose and out through the mouth, six times per day, especially right before bed.

- (Optional) Sleep Restriction – This practice exercise definitely is harder to implement because initially your sleep deprivation will almost certainly worsen. The two main keys to this exercise are limiting yourself initially to the amount of time you estimate you're staying asleep (not just laying in bed) and increasing that amount by increments of 15 minutes until you reach 8 hours (or the amount at which you feel fully rested).

- Meditation – For the final practice exercise in this chapter (and the *Body* section), I ask you to engage in meditation, a fitting crossover activity to the next section, *Mind*. Remember that many options exist for meditation; I included a simple 2 minute guided meditation script for your use (and adaptation, if you wish). I encourage you to try it daily for a couple of weeks and see if you notice a difference in how you're feeling physically, mentally, and/or emotionally.

## **Part 2 Mind**: Step 4 Emotion Regulation

A critical component of true happiness is awareness of our self-talk and whether it is helping or hurting our wellbeing. In this chapter, I discussed use of cognitive behavioral therapy and positive psychology techniques to modify our self-talk. I closed the chapter with a discussion of the impact of self-confidence.

## Practice Exercise Checklist

- Pleasurable Activities – As part of a concept called behavioral activation, retroactively identify and log all of your pleasurable activities from the prior week, noting the day/date, pleasurable activity itself, and the length of time of the activity. Hopefully, there is at least one activity every day, but if not, the next practice exercise addresses that.

- Fun Activity Commitment – Armed with the knowledge from the first practice exercise, make a commitment to engage in more pleasurable activities than you did in the prior week, and a minimum of one per day. Note all of these activities, ideally trying for a mix of solo activities and social activities.

- Thought Log – Begin tracking, for at least two weeks, every situation where you experienced a negative emotion, noting the following: situation, emotion, emotional intensity, and thoughts preceding or occurring during the situation. This will help you to identify your unhelpful thoughts and thought patterns.

- Thought Challenging – This practice exercise is probably one of the toughest in book, let alone in this *Step*. Your goal is to challenge the thoughts identified in your Thought Log by asking yourself if the thoughts are accurate and/or helpful and then identifying more balanced thoughts, likely taking another perspective.

- Positive Emotions – Consider your feelings about your past, present, and future, as well as your feelings about your relationships and activities. The goal is to develop positive emotions in all of these areas and this practice exercise will help you in determining where to focus your energy.

- Positive Individual Traits – Time to identify and consider your use of your character strengths. This multi-part practice exercise asks you to go online and take a strengths test and then consider how you do or do not use those strengths in your everyday activities. Ultimately your goal is to use your positive individual strengths every single day.

- Applying Positive Psychology – You want to thrive, not just survive. Consider why you engage in the activities you do, whether work or play. Brainstorm ways to modify, adapt, or replace activities that are not using your highest strengths and giving you a sense of fulfillment and connection to the world.

- Overcoming Fear of Failure – The final practice exercise of the chapter asks you to pick an activity, big or small, you've procrastinated doing out of fear of failure. After identifying the activity (or a small chunk of it to start with), you are then to apply the nine steps to assist you with actually accomplishing that activity and moving forward successfully.

## Step 5 Who Are You?

Authenticity necessitates challenging you to consider whether who-you-are is who-you-want-to-be. This involved considering authenticity within yourself, finding your purpose, developing a life plan in support of that purpose, and taking those initial steps, whether big or small, in support of that plan.

## Practice Exercise Checklist

- Identifying the Mask – In order to live a full, authentic life we first need to identify our lack of authenticity. This practice exercise encourages you to directly question why you do what you do, both now and in the past.

- Discovering Authenticity – Taking the answers from the Identifying the Mask practice exercise and delving deeper, now consider how you act around others, when you're happiest, what kind of self-talk you engage in, and analyzing your surface roles.

- Finding Your Purpose – A big piece to living authentically is to determine what activity would bring you the most happiness. Consider your childhood dreams, your current daydreams, and what you (maybe secretly!) have always wanted to do.

- Dreaming Big – Obviously, implementing your dreams will have a huge impact on your life. While ideally this is mostly for the good, if you are now considering making a change, it can be helpful to consider how that change will possibly impact your current work and career; play or pleasurable activities; relationships; and finances.

- Creating Your Life Plan – Finally, put everything together, using relevant answers from earlier practice exercises to assess yourself, find your bliss, make a beginning plan, and take a first step toward living the life of your dreams.

## Step 6 Planning

If you don't have a plan to accomplish your goals, it really is just wishful thinking with little chance of success. As planning is the process by which you can accomplish your goals, I described goal-setting and development, effective time management, and the role of motivation in our goal development and achievement.

## Practice Exercise Checklist

- Imagining Your Ideal Life – Trying to identify goals, especially long-term goals, can be daunting, so this first practice exercise asks you to consider what your ideal life would look like and what some potential long-term goals could be developed from that idea.

- Short-Term Goals – Since long-term goals likely consist of large goals, and probably multi-step goals, this is where short-term goals come in. Identify short-term goals related to your long-term goal(s).

- Identifying Parts of Your Goal – Using your answers to the above practice exercises, begin the intellectual process of moving from identifying the problem in your life you're looking to solve, breaking it down into its pieces, and visualizing what it would look like to solve.

- Creating a To-Do List – Moving from developing goals to actually accomplishing them, consider the most powerful tool of them all – the to-do list. Write down the items on today's list, making certain that there are items related to your short- and long-term goals, in addition to unrelated but necessary needs.

- Understanding Motivation – Pick a goal and then ask yourself questions about your motivation for attaining that goal. Include visualizing the goal, options for attaining the goal, and activities you enjoy that may help you toward your goal.

- Maintaining Motivation – The final practice exercise of the chapter has two pieces. One, consider what has caused your motivation to flag in the past and what you did to overcome that. Two, consider what may cause your motivation to lapse while pursuing your current goal and some options that may help to overcome them.

## **Part 3 Spirit** : Step 7 Community

Returning to the topic of positive psychology, I discussed the importance of a meaningful life in being happy and increasing your sense of belonging in the world. The importance of volunteering for both personal and community development concluded the chapter.

## Practice Exercise Checklist

- Friends and Family Connections – Outside of ourselves, the first connections to consider and strengthen are with your friends and family. Consider who your closest friends and family are and, importantly, how much interaction you actually have with them.

- Neighborhood Connections – Then move up a societal level to consider how involved you are in your neighborhood. To make a neighborhood more than just a collection of houses, this type of involvement can be critical, even if it's just learning your neighbors' names.

- City/Town Connections – Moving up another societal level, consider your involvement within your city or town. Are you able to identify anything? The higher up the levels we go, typically the more challenging it is to identify connections.

- State and National Connections – People rarely consider their involvement at the state or national societal levels (let alone the international level), so this practice exercise asks you to consider ways in which you currently are connected at these levels. As with the other levels, if you find yourself struggling, consider the suggestions made for increasing connections.

- Volunteer Assessment – Volunteering is beneficial for ourselves and our community. This practice exercise asks you to consider what volunteering you currently do, big and small, structured or unstructured. If you aren't currently volunteering, the follow-up is to identify the barriers and begin to problem solve.

- Identifying Volunteer Opportunities – The final practice exercise of the chapter asks you to brainstorm three possibilities for volunteering, not with the expectation that you'll necessarily do all of them, but as a place to start for identifying at least one that you can do regularly.

## Step 8 Spirituality & Mindfulness

Beginning with a bold statement that spirituality is vital to happiness, I first defined religious spirituality and secular spirituality. Taking a broader view of spiritual connection, I then discussed mindfulness, minimalism, and gratitude as methods for connecting with ourselves and others.

## Practice Exercise Checklist

- Spiritual Identification – Belief in something bigger than the self is innately connected to happiness. This practice exercise asks you to consider your spiritual satisfaction and offers steps to make changes if appropriate.

- Mindfulness Assessment – Consider how in-the-moment you are by answering a series of basic questions just where you are, reading this chapter. Many people find themselves thinking about the past or the future instead of simply enjoying today's moments.

- Increasing Mindfulness – Once you've identified your basic level of mindfulness, repeat a modified version of the Mindfulness Assessment once an hour for all the hours you're awake in a 24 hour period. Note the thoughts going through your mind and the physical sensations, repeating the assessment as needed to increase your ability to stay focused in a given moment.

- Implementing Minimalism – Consider what you have in your life and whether it contributes to your happiness. There are three steps to assess and reduce physical belongings, time commitments, and technology overload, as appropriate to your individual lifestyle.

- Going to the Movies – What we choose to focus on has such an impact on emotion, this practice exercise asks you to read a story and then retell it in your own words, noting whether you mostly focused on the positive events in the story or the negative.

- Gratitude Journal – The final practice exercise of the chapter asks you to write down at least three things big or small that you were grateful for during the day. By keeping the journal for **at least** a couple of weeks (longer if possible) you'll find the recognition of these positive things, and expression of thanks if another person was involved, becomes your new automatic habit.

## Step 9 Trust

I concluded the *9 Steps* with the idea that trust is at the core of human society. I offered guidance and specific recommendations on ways to build trust in yourself and with others, including recognizing the role of taking others' perspectives and learning to forgive ourselves and others.

## Practice Exercise Checklist

- Trusting Yourself – Three not-so-simple questions begin the first practice exercise, designed to encourage you to accurately assess your own degree of trust in yourself. If you are unable to trust yourself, either because you do not believe yourself to be trustworthy or actually are not trustworthy, then you must work on that before working to build trust with others.

- Perspective Taking – The second practice exercise begins with the premise that perspective taking is one basic technique for increasing trust in almost any situation. Recognizing this may be challenging, trying to understand where another is coming from will result in increased goodwill for yourself and for others.

- Indicators of Trust – One way to assess your level of trust in others is to track your interactions with people for a week and note any physical or emotional changes, particularly unpleasant changes, occurring during the encounter. The more you experience discomfort, the more it suggests distrust of the people with whom you are interacting.

- Thoughts Related to Trust – Although asked only to answer nine true-or-false statements without overanalyzing your responses, your answers highlight your perceptions of your personal world and the people who populate it. If your instinctual answers to the questions suggest this is an area in need of development, pay attention to that.

- Trusting to Connect – This practice exercise gauges how trusting you are (as well as how trustworthy others may view you). You are asked to rate each of your most important relationships on how connected you feel to them. Your answers shine a light on how connected and thus trusting and trusted you are.

- Improving Trust in Yourself – Flip a coin when you're struggling to make a decision between two options. The catch is that you evaluate and make your choice based on how you feel once you know your random outcome. The goal is that over time you will increase your trust in your gut instincts.

- Forgiving to Build Trust – Being able to forgive is intimately connected to increasing trust in yourself and others. Actively taking the perspective of three people who have wronged you, you can begin to practice the idea of assumed benevolence.

- Modifying Thoughts to Improve Trust – The final practice exercise of the chapter asks you to again track your interactions with people for another week. This time, you are asked to actively work on modifying the way you're thinking about and interpreting the situations, such that over time you will notice fewer physical and emotional indicators of distrust.

## How Far Have You Come?

Having refreshed your memory on the *9 Steps to Authentic Happiness*, I'd like you to go back to the beginning again. Seriously. I humbly request that you return to the *Introduction* and retake the pre-test. Answer all the questions, score it as described, and then compare your overall happiness score and individual *Step* scores with the scores you had the first time you took the pre-test. Did any or all of the numbers increase? If they did, wonderful. If they did not, take a look at what did not improve (or even went down). Return to those *Steps* and reread those chapters, focusing on internalizing the information and applying the recommendations provided. Continue the process of moving forward.

And now I leave you with final words of wisdom, the beauty of which are self-evident:

*When I was five years old, my mother always told me that happiness was the key to life. When I went to school, they asked me what I wanted to be when I grew up. I wrote down "happy". They told me I didn't understand the assignment and I told them they didn't understand life.*

John Lennon

DR. HEATHER SILVIO

# ABOUT THE AUTHOR

Heather is the author of the six-book *Paranormal Talent Agency* series, the romantic comedy *Not Quite Famous: A Romantic Comedy of an Actress on the Edge*, the short story and poetry collection *Beyond the Abyss: Tales of the Supernatural*, the therapy book *Stress Disorders: A Healing Path for PTSD*, and the psychological thriller/murder mystery *Courting Death*. A licensed clinical psychologist, actress, and law enforcement trainer, she lives in Las Vegas with her wonderful husband, Sidney, and their goofy cat, Snowball.

To check out all this and more, as well as sign up for Heather's monthly newsletter, visit http://www.heathersilvio.com.

www.ingramcontent.com/pod-product-compliance
Lightning Source LLC
Chambersburg PA
CBHW020419010526
44118CB00010B/329